*Fully Connected* is a timely reminder to leaders at all levels to take time out to focus on themselves. Leaders are missing a big opportunity in expending significant time and energy to support others to thrive. If their wellbeing is not in play, their risk of burnout increases. With the rapidly accelerating pace of change in today's business world, now is the time for leaders to take action and connect with themselves.

> Janelle Delaney, Partner and Executive Sponsor for Women@IBM, IBM Australia

In a world addicted to constant chaos and relentless hustling, *Fully Connected* is a great reminder that making time for self-care and honouring all aspects of your life makes you a better all-round human — at work and home. Let's ditch the busyness and burnout for balance. Filled with tips to transition you to a fully connected state, this book is a must-read for anyone wanting to take back their power and find out what really makes them tick.

> Sarah Smith, Chief of Staff, Office of the Queensland Chief Entrepreneur

If there was ever a time for a book like this, it's now. After two years of Covid lockdowns and remote working, it can feel harder than ever to be fully connected with ourselves and our people. This book is a great reminder of the importance of taking time out to be fully connected and practical ideas you can put in place to make it happen. The book draws on a collection of stories, research and personal experiences. These are combined with reflection questions to take you on a journey of discovery which Mel articulates with humour and fun. I recommend this book if you are looking for ways to feel more *Fully Connected* with yourself and those around you.

**Michelle van Raalte, Continuous Improvement Lead, Complaint Transformation, ANZ**

Sometimes a book comes along that is a perfect fit for the times. One with a clear and coherent message that at once diagnoses a challenge that many are confronting while at the same time prescribing practical solutions that can actually be implemented. *Fully Connected* is just such a book. It is useful for leaders, aspiring leaders, or anyone simply seeking connection, meaning or a way to find a more personally sustainable path through life. Mel's writing is easy to read, insightful, and nuanced. In short, *Fully Connected* is a pleasure to read and has the potential to help you take a step towards being your best self.

**John Barton, Director and Chief Executive Officer, MGD**

Part-warm hug, part-friendly push in the right direction, Mel has done a great job pulling together the best thinking on leader effectiveness into one book. A succinct, funny, and practical read for any leader who knows they need to lead themselves before they can successfully lead others.

**Steph Clarke, facilitator; host of Steph's Business Bookshelf podcast.**

Every leader needs to read this book. Mel shares her wisdom generously and provides lots of practical tips to help everyone proactively live the life they want.

**Annie Bryce, CEO, Edge Early Learning**

Dear Intrepid Reader, the most truthful thing I can say about this book is that Mel has been gently persuading me to follow its ideas for the past ten years. She's been trying out this material on me and, I suspect, many others. Certainly not in a sneaky way. Rather, because she really knows what the f*&^ she's talking about. So, her advice and guidance springs forth naturally and with clarity. Reading this book, I saw many of the same questions she has asked me with genuine curiosity to help me deeply connect with what I love, what I'm good at, and what really adds value to my clients.

Bravo, Mel.

**Jen Dainer, Business Owner, GDI Strategies and Industrial Photo & Video**

*Fully Connected* is a warm-hearted wake-up call for leaders who feel disconnected from themselves, their team members, and their work. Mel Kettle leads the way to becoming a connected leader through her open and honest reflections. She walks us through how to put ourselves first, and how taking care of ourselves will help us to take care of and lead our teams. It is a must-read for those of us who need to stop giving too much, take a step back and focus on what's important — ourselves.

**Angela McDonald, Managing Director, Optimum Recoveries**

This book couldn't have come at a better time! Women business owners and leaders know how to juggle, but the post-pandemic world has stretched even the most dextrous. Mel Kettle's ability to connect with those around her, and to cut through the layers of complications and challenges make *Fully Connected* a relatable and workable guide to reclaiming the joy in our lives. It's a contemporary survival guide — for women and for all leaders.

**Cheryl Gray, CEO, Women's Network Australia**

It can be a pressure cooker and lonely at the top. For experienced and emerging leaders, Mel's latest book is a treasure trove of practical, interesting and behaviour-changing advice on authentic leadership and how to stay fully connected. Focusing on what you can control (including yourself), and staying in the moment when things get tough, is the art of a high-achieving professional tennis player. It is also the art of great leadership, as Mel explains so eloquently in *Fully Connected*.

**Mark Woodrow, Customer Success Leader and IABC APAC Board Member**

# Fully Connected

Also by Mel Kettle:

*The Social Association*

# Fully Connected

How great leaders prioritise themselves,
reclaim their energy and find joy

**MEL KETTLE**

Published by Mel Kettle
First published in 2022 in Queensland, Australia

Copyright ©Mel Kettle
www.melkettle.com

The moral rights of the author have been asserted.

All rights reserved, except as permitted under the Australian Copyright Act 1968 (for example, fair dealing for the purposes of study, research, criticism or review). No part of this book may be reproduced, stored in a retrieval system, communicated or transmitted in any form or by any means without prior written permission from the author.

This book uses stories to enforce the meaning behind its relevant chapter. Permission to use these stories has been provided. In some cases, names have been changed.

Edited by Jenny Magee

Typeset and printed in Australia by BookPOD

ISBN: 978-0-6482541-2-6 (paperback)
ISBN: 978-0-6482541-3-3 (ebook)

For Shaun.

Who supports all my ideas, even when I'm sure he is thinking 'not another one'.

I love you. x

# About the Author

Mel Kettle is an internationally recognised thought leader on fully connected leadership and communication.

She is a trusted mentor to executives and leaders, and a highly sought-after speaker and trainer. Her clients include leaders, teams and organisations that want to achieve real connection and sustained engagement.

At the heart of everything Mel does is a commitment to self-leadership. She has an over-arching belief that we need to lead ourselves first before we can lead others. This view came after she survived the debilitating effects of work-related loneliness, stress and burnout in her late twenties and was reinforced by a life-threatening melanoma in her early forties.

Mel has written *Fully Connected* for leaders who want to take back ownership of their life, reclaim their health and energise their workforce.

Recognised by the leadersHum community as one of the Top 200 Biggest Voices in Leadership to watch for in 2022, Mel is one of only seven Australians on that list.

Mel is also the founder of the award-winning menopause blog, *Just as Juicy* (www.justasjuicy.com).

Mel loves to cook, dance around the house, and read crime thrillers in her spare time.

*Fully Connected* is Mel's second book.

**www.melkettle.com**

# Acknowledgements

The ideas within this book started floating around my mind many years ago. I wasn't sure it was the right book for me to write, despite knowing that it could make a difference. It's a big departure from much of what I am known for, and it couldn't be more different from my first book, *The Social Association*.

Part way through 2019, I started to tease out some of the ideas captured in these pages with clients, friends and colleagues through social media posts, newsletters and blogs. The feedback indicated that what I was saying resonated, and there were requests for more.

This book would not have been written without those who asked for more. Those of you who liked, commented on and shared my content, subscribed to my newsletter, booked me to speak at your conferences, run workshops and training with your teams, and asked for mentoring and coaching. Thank you.

Thank you also to the people who helped me get this book out of my head and onto paper.

My friend and mentor Lisa O'Neill told me I *must* write this book because I had things to say that people needed to hear. My book coach, the fabulous Kelly Irving, held my hand as I completely re-wrote the first version and tweaked and improved the many, many subsequent versions. My editor Jenny Magee removed 137 exclamation marks (!) and smoothed out my clunky language, so it read more easily. Sylvie Blair and her publishing team at BookPOD made self-publishing seem effortless.

An enormous thank you to my beautiful friends Louisa Coppel and Julia Steel. There aren't enough words to say how much I cherish our friendship and your loving support. You have been with me every step of the way with this book (and with life in general), helping me work through ideas and asking the hard questions (always with love). You remind me why I'm doing this. I love you both and can't wait to see you again.

Thank you also to my Book Stars crew for cheering me on – Monique Beedles, Winitha Bonney, Kate Bourke, Stephen Duns, Justine Figo, Joe Hart, Ganapathy Iyer and Karen Livey. I'm looking forward to celebrating our book-writing achievements in person.

This book wouldn't be as interesting without clients and colleagues who shared their stories. Many are included within the book. Please be assured that some names have been changed to protect the innocent (and the not-so-innocent) and where confidentiality has been required or requested. Thank you, especially to Mark Anderson, Fiona Brown, Debra Cerasa, Jason Laird, Catherine Medhurst, Aaron Newman, Kim Stockham, Sharon Tuffin, Tracy Whitelaw and Ben Vasiliou.

To my clients over the past sixteen years: it's been quite a ride, and it's nowhere near over yet. Thank you for entrusting me with your hearts, your souls and your people.

To family and friends who have been in the background: happy to distract me with a chat, a meal, a gin or cup of tea, while gently encouraging me to persevere with this book. Thank you, especially to Julian, Emma, Zoe and Sam Kettle, Jen Dainer, Jo Bargon, Anita Heiss, Collette Barton-Ross, Aisha Barton-Ross, Angela McDonald, Leanne Hughes, Susan Lambe, Sally Bagshaw, Ingrid Larkin, Kirsten Binnie, Dyan Johnson, Alisha Lynch, Mark Woodrow, Frederique Blanc, Jennifer Johnston, Bec Chappell and Michelle Scheibner. Many others are not mentioned but gratefully acknowledged.

This book was written over many cups of tea and coffee, countless gin and tonics, and numerous bottles of wine. It would be remiss not to thank the café owners in Brisbane and Caloundra who let me sit quietly and write while drinking their coffee.

Thank you to Shaun. My love. As I said in my previous book, you might roll your eyes when I say, 'I've been thinking...', but you always listen. And you have always believed in me, even when I have had doubts.

Finally, thanks to you, my readers, for choosing to read this book. For being willing to take a deeper look into who you are and what you stand for. If you want to let go of what isn't right in your life to become fully connected, then I hope this book helps you achieve that.

# Contents

Introduction     1

## Part One
## Connect With Yourself

Chapter 1: It's Time To Lead Yourself First     9

Chapter 2: From Surviving To Thriving     35

## Part Two
## Prioritise Yourself

Chapter 3  Become More Self-aware     67

Chapter 4: Become Self-motivated and Take Action     105

Chapter 5: Prioritise Self-care     135

Final words     171

References and Reading     173

Want more?     177

Endnotes     179

# Introduction

## Lessons from the best

In April 2022, along with fans worldwide, I was dumbfounded to hear that the currently ranked world number one women's tennis player, Ash Barty, was retiring. At twenty-five years of age. And at the top of her game.

Unless you're a tennis fan, you may not know what makes Ash Barty so beloved. More than her tennis prowess, it's her whole attitude to life. Late in 2014, she decided to take a break from tennis so she could do 'more teenage girl things'. She was recruited to play semi-professional cricket, even with no formal training in this sport. Barty returned to tennis in early 2016 and, in June 2019, became the top women's tennis player in the world. Her reign lasted 121 weeks.

On hearing of her retirement, I felt sad because I wouldn't get to watch her play again, and then I thought, 'Wow, what a champion!'.

Leaving the game on her terms. Putting *herself* first.

Barty announced her decision on Instagram in conversation with her close friend Casey Dellacqua, saying, 'I know in my heart, for me as a person, this is right'.

We face challenging decisions every day, and our choices are often based on what works for other people and what's right for them.

Hearing a woman as loved and respected as Ash Barty announce that she is fine if people don't understand her decision because *she* is okay with it, is inspiring. She said, 'It was hard, but it's right, and that brought me comfort, knowing it's right for me'.

Ash commented that her perspective shifted after winning Wimbledon in July 2021. She realised that her happiness wasn't dependent on the results, the money, or the status that winning provided. Her metric of success was not based on whether she won or lost. It depended instead on whether she gave everything she could.

If Ash Barty can connect to put herself first, prioritise her needs, and not be fussed about whether the general public understands her decision, then why can't we?

Leaders today are exhausted and frustrated. They know there is more to life than the treadmill on which they find themselves, but they aren't quite sure how to get it.

Too many leaders don't look after themselves. They exist in survival mode, struggling with unnecessary stress, overwhelm and burnout – but unfortunately, many don't realise this until it's too late. Add to this the past two years of Covid, which have left people scared, anxious and often disconnected. Despite endless Zoom meetings!

Great leaders value their people. They want to know how to encourage them to turn up ready to do a good day's work while being happy and healthy.

Leaders know they need to lead by example but aren't always sure what that looks like. In many cases, they don't believe they have the time to prioritise themselves.

I wrote this book because life is really bloody short. I see far too many people squander opportunities and trivialise what they have and who they are because they don't believe in themselves. They don't recognise they have choices and don't feel they are good enough to make them.

I want you to understand that:

- you are worth it
- you can back yourself
- you should prioritise yourself.

I want you to know:

- what lights you up
- when and how to say no to what doesn't bring you joy (or lead to something that will)
- when to say yes to what scares you
- how to set boundaries so you can live your best life.

# Connecting with yourself

What does connection mean to you?

I put this question to every guest on my podcast, *This Connected Life*.[1]

While everyone has a different answer, there are common themes.

*Connection is a two-way relationship between people.*

*Connection is a willingness or a shared agreement to be vulnerable.*

*Connection is not about what you're doing, it's about who you are being.*

*Connection starts with you. If you're not connected to yourself, how can you be connected to others?*

Before we can be connected to others, we need to be connected to ourselves. We need to know what makes *us* tick. We need to put ourselves first.

I believe human connection is the single most important element of life. It is vital for our physical, mental and emotional wellbeing, providing us with happiness, a sense of security and support.

Being connected doesn't mean having the most connections on LinkedIn, the most friends on Facebook, or the most

## FULLY CONNECTED

Twitter followers. It means having real, deep, human relationships.

This book will help you become fully connected, to take back ownership of your life, reclaim your health, and find joy.

As you read, reflect on what you want from life and think seriously about how you can take action to achieve it.

Life is short. You only get one chance. Please live it.

Mel x

June 2022

*Fully Connected* is written in two parts.

In Part One, we'll look at why you need to connect with yourself and lead yourself first. How can you bring your best when looking after or serving others if you don't look after yourself? Unless we connect first with ourselves, we risk unnecessary stress, overwhelm and burnout. Part One explores the reasons and benefits of becoming fully connected.

Part Two is all about prioritising yourself. It's not always easy to put yourself first, but it's worth it. This section identifies the three essential steps to prioritise you, find joy, and reclaim your energy. It's full of practical tools and suggestions to help you believe in yourself, take the necessary actions and thrive.

Before you start reading, I encourage you to download the accompanying workbook from www.melkettle.com/fullyconnected.

The workbook includes checklists, questions and practical exercises for each chapter that will help you apply what you learn.

# Part One

# Connect With Yourself

It is more important than ever to connect with ourselves. Leadership – and life – is getting harder, making it increasingly difficult to find the time and energy to put ourselves first. We must look after our health and wellbeing to bring our best selves to work.

Self-care isn't selfish. Yet when we face increased pressures with work and life, it can be hard to put ourselves first.

Too often, we are afraid of others' reactions to our vulnerability. Add to this the growing epidemic of loneliness negatively impacting our health and increasing the risk of anxiety and depression. Is it any wonder we so often struggle to connect with ourselves?

The noise and pressure of technology and social media also challenge our ability to filter out the unwanted and unhelpful. And then, of course, we are dealing with the ongoing impact of Covid-19. All of which contribute to our lack of connection with ourselves and others.

Fully connected leaders thrive.

They take back ownership of their lives, reclaim their health and have stronger relationships. They energise their workforce, communicate with conviction and create cultures of belonging.

Part One explores how you can do this in detail.

# Chapter One

# It's Time To Lead Yourself First

*To live is the rarest thing in the world.
Most people exist, that is all.*

– Oscar Wilde

A few years ago, I went overseas for a seven-week holiday. On my own.

I would love to have shared at least part of it with my husband, Shaun, as was our initial plan, but that didn't end up happening – for a lot of boring reasons. When we realised Shaun couldn't come, I thought (for a nano-second) about cancelling. My clients had been alerted months earlier, and my schedule was clear.

It was one of the best experiences of my life. Although not for the reasons you might expect.

This trip was planned so that every second week I would catch up with family and friends – ten days in Paris, ten days in the UK and a week in San Francisco. In the middle of this holiday, I had a week on my own in Istanbul – a city I had long wanted to visit.

My excitement about visiting Istanbul should have been off the charts, and, on one level, it was. However, I also felt despondent and unsettled, and I couldn't understand why. In theory, I had it all – a loving partner, a beautiful home, a successful business with many fabulous clients.

In hindsight (always wonderfully clear), I was struggling with anxiety and probably bordering on depression. I was still grieving the unexpected deaths of my parents a few years earlier, and a values misalignment with my biggest client was causing significant inner conflict.

To top it all off, I was in the throes of perimenopause, which I didn't realise because no one had ever talked about it.

For those who are unsure, perimenopause is the time before a woman goes through menopause. It's a hormonal change that happens to all women who reach fifty-ish. It usually starts in our forties (or even thirties) and can last more than fifteen years. Yep, that's right. Fifteen years of symptoms that include: anxiety, depression, panic attacks, weight gain, short-term memory loss, hot flushes, night sweats, difficulty sleeping, lack of self-esteem, crankiness, and joint pain. Most women don't have all these symptoms, but most of us have some. Please be kind to us during this time. And more importantly, if you're going through this now, be kind to yourself.

Okay, back to my story.

Given all that, it's not surprising I was so perturbed. It was also the first time in twenty years that I'd had a significant amount of time to stop and focus only on myself. I had been busy starting and quickly building a meaningful career, doing two post-graduate degrees, moving to a new city (twice), meeting Shaun, setting up our home together, and quitting my job to launch my business.

This holiday came at precisely the right time. It was a chance to put myself first. To do what I loved. To reconnect with myself.

So much of my life until then had been spent prioritising other people, doing what they wanted and expected. I had forgotten who I was, what I wanted and what made me happy.

## Connecting with strangers

One of the greatest opportunities when travelling alone is our conversations with strangers. It's especially so when we open ourselves up to deeper conversations than we might have with people who already know us. There's a beautiful sense of freedom in making a meaningful connection with someone you know you will never see again.

One such random conversation helped me understand why I was feeling so discombobulated.

My day of revelation started with sunshine, which was a welcome change after a few cold, wet and miserable days. It was time to explore Istanbul properly.

I jumped on a bus heading north of the city, following the Bosphorus, the strait that separates the European from the Asian part of Turkey. Also on the bus were two young American Jehovah's Witnesses who had recently moved to Istanbul to be missionaries for a year. We started chatting, and they mentioned they were heading to the annual Istanbul Tulip Festival. Never one to miss a good festival, I invited myself to tag along.

We spent most of the day together, with incredibly thought-provoking conversations about religion, belief and connection. Without getting too woo-woo, I genuinely believe the universe provides what you need when you need it. Sometimes, you need to stop and look, but your answer will always be there.

This day was the universe providing for me. This chance meeting and our conversations about life and prioritising what you love helped me better understand the importance of putting myself first. It made me rethink meeting my needs, looking after my health, and taking time to recharge my body, soul and mind. And the importance of doing this regularly and frequently.

When reflecting later, I realised that while I had great connections with others, I wasn't at all connected to myself. This young couple helped me understand that continually putting other people's needs and priorities ahead of mine tells me that I don't matter. And if I don't believe I matter, then why should anyone else?

I returned home from this holiday with a renewed sense of self.

The changes made me a better person and a better leader. I had more energy, my relationships with my clients improved, and I became more focused.

When we connect with ourselves first, we are happier, healthier and more human.

## You first

As leaders, we have a responsibility to care for ourselves first. A lot of livelihoods rely on us.

Putting yourself first is so important. If you don't look after yourself, you can't be your best self for others. That includes your kids, partner, other family members, friends, employees, colleagues, boss and anyone else who is important in your world.

> Putting yourself first is so important.

Too many leaders don't look after themselves, which means they struggle with unnecessary stress, overwhelm and burnout. Many don't realise this is happening until they take a break from work (as I did), or worse, they find out too late.

Of course, it's hard to have downtime if you work in an organisation that subscribes to what Anne-Marie Slaughter calls our time macho culture: 'A relentless competition to work harder, stay later, pull more all-nighters, travel around the world and bill the extra hours that the international date line affords you'.[2]

Is it any wonder that so many of us are struggling?

I speak with many CEOs and other senior executives who say:

'It's really lonely at the top. I didn't expect that.'

'I sometimes feel that change is the only constant, and it's overwhelming.'

'I'm being pulled in so many directions that I can't remember which way is up.'

'Everyone wants a piece of me – my staff, my board, our customers, my wife, my kids. I don't have any time for myself.'

'I feel like I'm on a never-ending cycle of stress, alcohol, not sleeping and anxiety meds, and I don't know how to stop it.'

'I cry in the car on my way home from work at least once a week.'

'Am I really cut out for this? The pressure is so much more than I ever expected, and I don't know if I want to be the boss anymore.'

'I dread Mondays.'

'How do I structure my life so that work doesn't crowd everything out? How can I find time for hobbies again?'

'I feel an overwhelming commitment to being dutiful and keeping others happy, and this is like a constant ball and chain around me.'

'I don't know how to say no, even to things I really don't want to do.'

'I'm so tired I can't think, which means I'm no longer confident that I'm making the right decisions.'

Sound familiar?

If we don't make time to connect with ourselves, look after our health and wellbeing, and work towards achieving our goals and priorities, how can we bring our best selves to work?

# Better for each other

As leaders, we want our people to turn up to work, ready to do their jobs to the best of their ability. We want them to gain satisfaction from a good day's work. We want them to be happy and healthy, and feel they can come to us when things aren't quite right – at work and home.

And they can't, or won't, do that if they don't know or understand what's expected or what they need to do or what's in it for them. Or if they don't like, respect or understand their manager, CEO or other leaders in your organisation. Or if they are exhausted, overwhelmed or stressed, and feel excluded or marginalised.

We can't expect our people to turn up and do their best if we aren't.

I know there are times when I have been a great leader and times when I have been shockingly awful. Looking back, I see that the terrible times were when my values or my purpose were not clear. I allowed other people's priorities to be the basis of my decisions, and I certainly didn't maintain any sort of self-care routine.

My first leadership role at work came in my late twenties. The headiness of being headhunted and winning the role over far more senior candidates meant I didn't do the necessary due diligence. I didn't even negotiate my salary because I didn't know I could! (That needs to be taught in high school. Seriously.)

I was well and truly thrown into the deep end, with no idea what I was getting into. My newly formed and enthusiastic team were all younger than me, and we learned the job together.

While I had the skills and capability to do the basics, I had no idea how to manage the people. I didn't want to ask for help because I didn't want my employer to realise I didn't know what I was doing. There was no training, so I muddled along. As time went by, we all became exhausted from the stress of the job, the long hours and the diverse and often difficult personalities of the many people we needed to work with.

Work kept piling up, and I realised I couldn't say no without risking my job. My boss was under even more pressure to perform, so there was little support at work, and no support at home, as I lived alone.

Given that I was not, in any way, bringing my best self to work, it's no surprise that relationships and communication with my team suffered. The lack of any real breaks (including proper sleep), poor nutrition and increasing anxiety meant I retreated into myself to survive.

It was a horrible time, and when I finally resigned, I vowed I would do better the next time I was given a leadership opportunity. While I know I wasn't the first bad leader, I definitely won't be the last. Part of the leadership experience is learning from past mistakes and doing better the next time.

I asked Sharon Tuffin, CEO of Karralika Programs, what she wished she had done differently as a younger leader. Her response was, 'I felt that I needed to prove myself, and so, wrongly, I didn't seek help. I believed that I needed to prove why I got this job, and why I had this level of responsibility. However, by assuming I could do it all myself, I didn't take advantage of the really great insights and experience of others in the organisation. I lost opportunities to learn and be challenged because I wasn't being true to myself.'

> We must become better versions of ourselves.

As we progress through our careers, we must become better versions of ourselves to be better leaders, at home, at work and within our communities.

## Why is it so hard to put ourselves first?

It's totally understandable that we put others first. After all, you want to invest in your people and help them feel safe and valued. Good leaders *want* to serve others. They *want* to create an organisational culture that is uplifting, motivating and instils confidence in their workforce.

We know that leaders have always faced challenges; however, they seem bigger and bolder these days. It feels like we have even more to do and less time than ever to do it. Add the increasing integration between work and life (not only because of Covid), and we must wonder whether we are working from home or living at work.

When I started my career in the mid-1990s, work-life balance was an ideology that many, including me, struggled to achieve. Computer technology had advanced to a point where we could more easily take our work out of the office. I remember how privileged I felt when my employer gave me my first laptop in 1999. Little did I know that it was the beginning of the end of my work-life separation. I worked, on average, seventy hours a week in that job, with barely a weekend when I didn't dial in from my home internet connection. (Do you remember that dial-up sound too?)

Today, working for myself gives me the flexibility to choose how, where and when I work. However, it also means I frequently find it hard to switch off. And yes, I'm writing this late on a Sunday afternoon, after a restorative yoga class and before starting to cook dinner and plopping on the couch to watch MasterChef.

I'm highly conscious that employees have fewer choices. A colleague recently told me she has senior executives call her at 2am, expecting to have a work-related conversation. She marvelled when I said that my phone is usually on silent from 8pm–8am. Her employer expects her to be available 24/7, which is simply not sustainable.

There are so many reasons it can be hard to take the time and effort to put ourselves first. I believe the following six are the main explanations.

## We have increased pressures with work and life

Even before Covid, leaders had been feeling increased pressure. We are so often over-scheduled and over-committed. Life is often further complicated by the notion that we need to be seen to be busy. When you ask someone how they are, how often is the reply 'I'm busy'?

> We glorify 'busy' far too often.

We glorify 'busy' far too often. It's not something to be proud of, yet so many are.

At work, we are expected to be available 24/7 and do more with less while motivating a frequently disengaged, multigenerational workforce. Changing customer expectations place greater demands on our workforce and our business models. Yet, we must maintain or increase organisational growth while staying competitive in increasingly disruptive markets.

I feel exhausted just writing this!

And let's not forget our responsibilities at home. We often juggle children and ageing parents while trying to find time for romance. Women, in particular, struggle with the mental load of endless tasks. It's the list-making, the planning and the organising that must occur every day to ensure you, the kids and your partner can get out the door in the morning. It's the decisions about what to have for dinner, where to go on the weekend, which movie to watch, who will look after your pets when you're away, who will make sure the bills get paid on time, buying birthday gifts, booking the plumber, the pest control, the car maintenance....

Coordinating these logistics to ensure life runs smoothly means we have less time to do things for ourselves and do what we love. It creates friction that saps our energy and can tip us into overwhelm.

## We mistake self-care for selfishness

It's so easy to put others' needs first and ignore your own – especially when the only person you're accountable to is yourself. This can be even truer for women, as we are often taught that it's inconsiderate or rude to put our needs before those of our partners, children and other family members.

Focusing time and energy on looking after yourself is often considered selfish.

Let me tell you: it is not.

Putting yourself first isn't only about caring for yourself. It's about understanding your most important priorities, and managing accordingly. Putting yourself first is often the best way to support everyone else.

## You need to be responsible for you.

It also recognises that *you* need to be responsible for *you*.

If you're going through perimenopause, it's even more important to focus on self-care. This stage of life can be incredibly isolating, not to mention frustrating. We all have different menopause experiences, so taking time to understand your specific needs will help you better manage this stage of life. Be gentle *and* patient with yourself as your body changes. And yes, this is often easier said than done....

If you don't look after yourself, why should anyone else?

In 2011, Michelle Obama was First Lady of the United States. In an interview, she told Barbara Walters that putting herself highest on her priority list wasn't selfish – it was practical. She said, '[Putting myself first is] something that I found I needed to do for quite some time, even before the presidency. And I found other women in similar situations, balancing career and family, trying to do it all. A lot of times, we just slip pretty low on our own priority list because we're so busy caring for everyone else. And one of the things that I want to model for my girls is investing in themselves as much as they invest in others.'[3]

## We're afraid of the reaction to our vulnerability

I'm sure I'm not the only one who has pushed through a bad situation at work because we don't want to show any sign of weakness for fear of being seen as incapable or worse. Sometimes, however, it just comes out. Like when my boss called to check in while I was running a huge project at a fancy hotel during Melbourne Cup Week.

I'm fairly sure he didn't expect me to burst into tears and sob until I hyperventilated. I know he cared – he called my colleague who was also in Melbourne and asked her to find me and make sure I was okay. However, he also expected me to pick myself up and complete the project, so I didn't let the client down. Back in the office the following week, he asked if I felt better, but nothing changed.

Then there was the time I told another boss I had too much on my plate at work, was getting extremely stressed about deadlines and couldn't get everything done. A promotion meant that sixty per cent of my time was spent with the new role (and a new boss) and forty per cent on my old role (and old boss). My old boss didn't like this, despite agreeing to the change. He told me that he expected me to still do all my former duties to the high standard he was used to. When I said there weren't enough hours in the week, he told me (and anyone who would listen) that I was lazy and useless.

I know I can't be the only person who has received a negative response to showing vulnerability or asking for help.

> Showing vulnerability can seem even more difficult.

When you're in charge, showing vulnerability can seem even more difficult. We can't expect our staff and colleagues to open up to us if we don't open up to them.

A few years ago, one of my CEO clients, Anna (not her real name), talked about a staff member whose performance was rapidly declining. She felt there was a problem with Brett's (not his real name either) home life, but numerous conversations had elicited nothing. I asked whether Brett was aware of the enormous personal challenges she was currently facing, and Anna said, 'No, of course not. I keep my personal life private'.

I asked her why Brett should be open with her when she was a closed book with him. I wasn't suggesting that Anna divulge all the nitty-gritty of her dramas, but that she gave her team a broad overview of what she was going through. I reminded her that disclosure breeds disclosure, and that if she shared some confidences, it might encourage Brett to open up. It would also help her team understand why she was occasionally distracted and abrupt – two behaviours that were not her normal but becoming more common as she grappled with major personal issues.

## There's a growing epidemic of loneliness

Loneliness has been at epidemic levels for a long time, with one in two Australians saying they are lonely at least once a week.[4]

Cigna's 2020 Loneliness Index shows a clear connection between work and loneliness, with sixty-one per cent of the study's respondents reporting they were lonely. Interestingly, the research shows that men were slightly more lonely than women, and younger people (aged 18–22) were lonelier than older people (72+).[5]

Many senior executives I've worked with have shared how lonely they've been at work. I certainly recall this from when I was in a senior role. I couldn't talk to my boss about it, in case she thought I wasn't up to the role. I couldn't discuss it with my team, as they expected me to have the answers. And my husband didn't understand as, at that stage, he hadn't been in a senior role. It wasn't a great time in my life.

Research by RHR International found that more than half of the CEOs studied reported feeling lonely in their job, with the majority believing it hindered their performance. This was particularly true for first-time CEOs.[6]

Leaders must understand that loneliness can have a considerable impact on health, ours and our staff, and the bottom line of our organisations.

If you have been in the workforce for a while, it will be no surprise to learn that we are twice as likely to say we are

> The impacts of loneliness are far-reaching.

always exhausted than we were twenty years ago. Almost half of us say this is due to work. There is also a significant correlation between work exhaustion and feeling lonely – the more you're exhausted, the more alone you feel. It's a vicious cycle that can be hard to stop.

The impacts of loneliness are far-reaching. Our cognitive performance and executive functions diminish. We have difficulty staying focused, listening and paying attention, planning and prioritising, recalling instructions, multitasking, and controlling our impulses. We also struggle to learn, think, reason, remember, problem solve and make decisions.

Loneliness also makes us more prone to anxiety and depression, which correlate directly with workforce engagement, productivity, and profit. When it comes to absence from work, depression and anxiety are now the leading causes of long-term sickness absence and a major cause of presenteeism.[7]

For many of my clients, friends and colleagues, the last two years have increased feelings of loneliness. Many who combined living alone with working from home often found the loneliness debilitating. As leaders, we need to carefully consider the impact of a hybrid workforce, especially on those who crave the return to the office and the company of others.

## We can't easily filter out the noise

Screen time isn't inherently bad. However, what is concerning is the amount of time we spend living our lives through the screen and not with people.

We need to be more deliberate about how and when we use technology.

One of the reasons we are disconnected is our love of screens. And yes, I mean that in the plural. The average Australian household has 6.4 screens,[8] including TVs, mobile phones, tablets and computers. Even my Thermomix is connected to the internet, although I can't yet use it to watch Netflix.

We check our phones around 340 times a day, which equates to once every four minutes. And each time we check, we are priming our brain for distraction for the rest of the day. That means we are hit with information overload and are unable to prioritise tasks. Reading a text message, which takes less than three seconds, can double error rates on basic tasks.[9] [10]

Our increase in screen time – toggling between apps, mindlessly scrolling, binge-watching the latest show on our streaming service of choice, and constantly checking social media and our inbox for updates – leads us to have shorter attention spans.[11]

It is also causing insomnia, worry and fatigue, which are precursors to burnout, anxiety and depression. Literacy and the ability to spell, be creative and think critically are declining. Cyberbullying and trolling are increasing.

Then there's the increase in physical ailments, such as text-neck, cyber-sickness, text-claw, phantom vibe, hearing loss, RSI and eye strain. The artificial blue light emanating from screens can lead to poor sleep and mood disorders, including depression and anxiety, and increase the risk of cancer, obesity, diabetes, and reproductive problems.

Many of us joke about being addicted to our phones, yet we carry them around as though they are EpiPens, and we all have a fatal illness. Despite the joking, it's a serious matter. Smartphone addiction is a definite thing, and it's becoming more and more prevalent as we choose phones over humans. A study from the University of Derby indicated that one in eight people are addicted to their phones.[12] It's hardly surprising, given the average Aussie spends 5.5 hours *every day* on their phone.

And it's not only our phones. We're increasingly addicted to streaming services, such as Netflix, Stan, Hulu, Apple TV+, Disney+ and Amazon Prime – not to mention the TV stations with their online services, such as SBS Online, ABC's iView and the rest.

Reed Hastings, CEO of Netflix, has said that the biggest competitor of Netflix is sleep. He said, 'When you watch a show from Netflix, and you get addicted to it, you stay up late at night. We're competing with sleep.'¹³

Think about that for a moment. And then consider your TV viewing habits.

And what about technology at work?

> **The biggest competitor of Netflix is sleep.**

We have email, which is the bane of many an office worker's life, with the average office worker receiving 121 emails *per day*.¹⁴ And we have Zoom fatigue, born of the hours and hours we spend in online meetings. One of the reasons video calls are so exhausting is because we need to focus far more intently than in-person or talking on the phone. Ironically, the extra attention required to focus on the other faces takes energy we don't use face-to-face. If we turn away on a video call, look down while taking notes, read through the meeting agenda, or glance at an incoming message on our phone, it seems as though we are no longer paying attention. So, we focus harder.

During one of the early Covid lockdowns, I was thrilled to see Heritage Bank announce boundaries around when their staff could have online meetings.

CEO Peter Lock said that as seventy per cent of their workforce were now working from home, they decided to introduce guidelines around Zoom, which included no meetings before 9.30am, between 12.30-1.30pm, after 4.30pm, or on Fridays. The purpose was to support people's mental health and ensure they could get work done, rather than always being 'on'. He hoped that by limiting meeting hours, staff would have time to walk the dog, exercise, have a proper lunch break and take some time each day to temporarily switch off.[15]

## Covid-19 has an ongoing impact

As we head into a new post-pandemic reality, we need to rethink our understanding of mental health and wellbeing.

You might be reading this in 2022 as we move through the pandemic or a few years later. Perhaps another event, personal or professional, has caused a significant change in your life. It might be an unexpected job loss, the death of a loved one, the end of a relationship, or a serious health challenge. Regardless of what life throws at you, remember that it's okay not to be okay.

The first episode of Brené Brown's podcast, *Unlocking Us*,[16] was released soon after the coronavirus was declared a global pandemic. She talked about the FFTs, 'the Fucking First Time' (sorry, not sorry, for swearing), reminding us that the first time of any new experience can be horribly difficult. First dates, the first time we get behind the steering wheel of a car, the first time we go through a global pandemic. And the first time we start thinking about a post-pandemic reality.

As leaders, we sometimes need to remind ourselves that first times can be hard. So, let's treat ourselves gently.

In a 2021 *New York Times* article, Adam Grant wrote that so many of us are languishing, referring to the joylessness and aimlessness we feel. It's that grey area between burnout and bouncing, between depression and flourishing. 'It feels as if you're muddling through your days, looking at your life through a foggy windshield,' said Grant.[17]

One of the problems with languishing is that you're 'indifferent to your indifference', which means you don't tend to seek help or try to help yourself.

There are plenty of ways to cope with languishing, including taking time out, doing things that bring joy and having a change of scene, which can be as simple as briefly stepping away from the office to get some fresh air.

As we connect with our colleagues, customers and others, it's important to remember that it's not just a significant event that can take its toll; it's the surrounding anxiety and the lack of joy and purpose.

## You only get one life

My unexpected favourite movie of the year a few years ago was *Jumanji: Welcome to the Jungle*. I was still laughing a week later. I recently watched it again and was reminded of how many positive messages about life it contains.

Without any spoilers, *Jumanji* is a video game (in the original movie with Robin Williams, it's a board game) that sucks its players into an alternate world to play a survival game. The only escape is by working together. The game is described as 'A game for those who seek to find a way to leave their world behind'.

At the start of the movie, the four main protagonists are sent to detention. Principal Bentley tells them: 'This is what you should be thinking about: Who you are ... in this moment of time ... and who you want to be. You get one life. You decide how you're gonna spend it. Fortunately ... there is no better place for self-reflection ... than detention.'

While in detention, they play *Jumanji* and find themselves in the jungle, where, as in all good video games, they have multiple lives.

Towards the end of the movie, Dr Smolder Bravestone comments, 'It's a lot easier to be brave when you've got lives to spare. It's a lot harder when you only have one life.' Moose Finbar replies, 'We always only have one life, man. That's how it is.'

## What about you?

My question is this. Are you living the life you want?

And if not, when will you make time for self-reflection?

Connecting with yourself is a conscious choice. We make decisions around this every day, about what we think, what we eat and drink, when we go to bed, who we associate with, and how we bring joy to our lives.

The only person who can work out what you want is *you*.

And the only person who can make the necessary change is – you guessed it – *you*.

## Are you living the life you want?

It's so easy to get caught up in our problems, forgetting we have choices in life. Every day we have the power to change our world. To make decisions that improve our quality of life in small and significant ways.

You now have a choice. Will you be a fully connected leader?

### Reflection questions

When did you last put yourself first?

_____

_____

_____

How did that make you feel?

_____

_____

_____

What is stopping you from putting yourself first more often?

_____

_____

_____

Are you living the life you want?

_____

_____

_____

What changes could you make?

_____

_____

_____

# Chapter Two

# From Surviving To Thriving

## If Karen can, so can you

Karen is a senior executive in a large company in the healthcare sector. When we met, she was juggling multiple responsibilities with her family, volunteering commitments, and job. Having spent much of her life and career putting the needs of others first, she was exhausted. Karen said it felt like she was barely surviving, and she wanted more. She wanted time for the things she loved and to make them a priority. But she didn't know how to fit anything else in.

Like many women in their late fifties, Karen had been raised to be useful and of service to others. The notion of putting herself first made her extremely uncomfortable. While her values included contribution, she was overcommitted as she found it difficult to say no to people who asked her to serve. She wanted to step away from some volunteering commitments but felt obligated to continue. This was partly because she had given her word, and she wanted to see some projects through to the end.

Karen was so used to putting other people first that she stopped investing in self-care. As a result, she felt unappreciated, undervalued, and unnecessarily stressed. These feelings negatively impacted her relationships at home and at work, as well as her ability to do her job to the high standards she set for herself.

We spent a lot of time working out her core values and priorities and identifying what lit her up and what dragged her down.

Over time, and with small steps, Karen made some changes. At work, she delegated more, restructured her calendar to include regular time for thinking, planning and undertaking deep work, and scheduled some annual leave. She said 'No thank you' to a request to be on another volunteer committee and developed a plan to step down from a board she served on. Karen started to create boundaries around how she spent her time and who she spent it with. And most importantly, she began to do more of the activities she loved. Regularly.

While Karen is still a work in progress (aren't we all?), she is well on the way to becoming the fully connected and thriving woman she wants – and deserves – to be.

Being fully connected is not only about caring for yourself. It's about understanding your most important priorities and managing them.

## Fully connected leaders

Self-awareness allows fully connected leaders to know and understand their values, attitudes and feelings. They have a clear purpose and the self-confidence to back themselves and create positive habits. And they recognise that self-care is critical to their success.

Fully connected leaders realise that connection to themselves is a commitment that takes time and energy and that this can be really f&*^ing hard.

Becoming fully connected is not an easy path. Doing the work, especially the inner work, can sometimes feel like climbing Everest. (Okay, so I've never climbed Everest and never really want to. But I have friends who have, and they say it's really hard. My current Everest is writing this chapter, which has been hell.) But it's worth it because fully connected leaders thrive.

When we are fully connected, we understand our fears and our flaws. We have a healthy approach to life and prioritise our physical, spiritual, emotional and mental health. We know what we stand for, and we motivate and inspire others.

Sounds pretty good, right?

## Stuck in survival mode

However, we must get out of survival mode before we can thrive.

Survival is when you're going through the motions to get through the day. You are completely overwhelmed with life and don't know where to turn. In a nutshell, survival mode is hell.

You overlook your own needs because everyone else's take priority.

You have forgotten what it feels like to be happy.

Everything is urgent, and you react to everything.

It's easier to do the job yourself rather than delegate.

You feel stressed to the max and have trouble sleeping. You self-medicate with caffeine, alcohol or worse. Your physical symptoms could include headaches, nausea, diarrhoea, feeling shaky, and sweating more than usual. You might even have chest pains. (If you do, go and get them checked out. Now.)

You really want to get out of this phase, but you don't know how to do so.

The first step is to recognise where you're at.

## Recognise where you're at.

I've been in survival mode a few times when I struggled to see the light at the end of the tunnel. It was hard and on some dark days, I wondered if it was all worth it. A chance conversation with my doctor made me realise there was hope and that I could take back control of my life – even though I was spiralling like an ice-skater in a constant spin.

The first thing I needed to do was acknowledge where I was, and that I wanted the situation to change. The first step in my road from surviving to thriving was reaching out for support. There is real truth in the expression 'a problem shared is a problem halved'. Conversations with my doctor and a trusted friend gave me the courage to talk to my boss about how I was feeling.

If you're currently feeling like you're in survival mode, understand that there is no quick fix. It takes time and effort to move from surviving to thriving. Picking up this book shows you recognise that something is wrong, and you want to fix it.

> A problem shared is a problem halved.

If you're in overwhelm right now, consider how you can do the following.

Reach out for support: Do you have a trusted doctor to talk to? Or can you connect with an employee assistance program?

Practice some simple grounding techniques: Walk barefoot on the grass, sit quietly and take several slow, deep breaths

Prioritise self-care basics: These might include sleep, eating the right foods, and even washing your hair. (There's more about self-care in Chapter Five.)

Talk about it: If the stress source is work-related, chat to your boss to identify core priorities and what can be put aside or delegated to someone else.

Do something you love every day – even if it's only for five minutes.

Once you have acknowledged how you're feeling, you can start to put one foot in front of the other to work your way back to thriving. You can start to take back control.

# Regaining control

A Chinese proverb says, 'The best time to plant a tree was twenty years ago, and the second-best time is now'.

It's the same with regaining control of your life. You wouldn't have lost control in a perfect world, but we don't live in a perfect world.

The first step in changing your circumstances is to recognise that something needs to change.

When I was a teenager, my father decided to stop drinking alcohol for a year. He recognised that slowly, over the years, his alcohol intake had started to creep up. It was the 1980s, and liquid lunches were common. It was also usual for him to have a beer to relax when he came home from work, a couple of glasses of wine with dinner and then maybe a digestif before bed. Dad had the slender physique and long legs (neither of which I inherited) of the middle-distance runner he had been in his youth. However, he noticed his clothing was a bit tight and that he was not as focused at work as he wanted – or needed – to be.

Dad wanted to break the cycle, so he, somewhat drastically, decided not to consume alcohol for a year. Within weeks he began to feel healthier, his clothes started to fit more comfortably, and he had a lot more energy. At the end of the year, he ended his alcohol fast but never returned to the quantity or frequency of previous years.

## Taking back ownership of your life

When we regain control, we take back ownership of our lives. We take responsibility for our actions, behaviours and decisions.

My friend Katrina is one of the most fully connected leaders I know. She is in her mid-forties, a senior executive, married, with one child. We have been friends for more than twenty years, and I have watched her grow and develop. When we met, she was uncertain about what she wanted from life and felt rather overwhelmed by the choices (as we so often are in our twenties). Like many twenty-somethings, Katrina worked hard and played hard.

A few years later, Katrina was on the cusp of burnout. She worked at least sixty hours a week in a job she didn't love and which required frequent, and often last minute, interstate travel. She was also newly married and keen to start a family. Katrina was aware that something had to change and she was prepared to make big decisions for the sake of her future.

Today Katrina works for a company that values family and supports flexible work conditions. She has done the hard work in growing her self-awareness and prioritising her self-care. Her team holds her in high regard, and not only because she leads by example when it comes to work-life integration. She genuinely cares about her colleagues and works hard to ensure they feel valued members of the organisation.

> When we are fully connected, we flourish.

Becoming fully connected is not easy, but it's worth the effort because the benefits are immense. When we are fully connected, we flourish. We are personally happier and healthier, and we are more human. These attributes have flow-on benefits, as we are now better equipped to energise our co-workers, communicate with conviction and create cultures of belonging.

Let's look at how.

## We are happier

Aristotle wrote, 'Happiness is the meaning and the purpose of life, the whole aim and end of human existence.'

Being happier is better for our personal lives, and research shows happy people are better workers. We are less stressed, live longer lives and are unwell less often. Happy people have a greater level of resilience and recover from illness more quickly, requiring fewer hospital visits and less medication.

> Research shows happy people are better workers.

They are more engaged and optimistic, and less likely to be absent. They are also more likely to have friendships with other employees, reducing feelings of loneliness at work.

When we are unhappy and disengaged, we are no fun to work with. Our moods and emotions impact us and those around us. The good news is that happiness is contagious. So, if you are feeling glum, spend some time with happy people, as this will positively impact your mood.

Happy people are also more successful, although the reverse is rarely true – success doesn't make us happy. Happiness has been linked to greater creativity, which is important for problem-solving, innovation, and finding new ways of doing things.

Increasingly, companies are investing in ways to make employees happy. One example is Google, whose investment in employee support has seen employee satisfaction increase by thirty-seven per cent. They found that higher employee happiness was associated with a twelve per cent rise in productivity.[18]

## We are healthier

A big part of being fully connected is knowing what's going on with our bodies and minds and looking after ourselves appropriately.

When we are physically, mentally and emotionally healthy, we feel better about ourselves, live longer, and are more capable of managing stress. We also have increased mental stamina and endurance, essential for effective leadership.

Healthy people have more energy and emotional stability, visit the doctor less and have fewer medical costs.

When we are healthier, we cost our companies less, with fewer absences from work, and are less inclined to presenteeism. We also have less impact on our colleagues, as the ripple effects from absences is reduced.

People with poor overall health take up to nine times more sick leave than their healthy colleagues, which has a significant impact on the bottom line. Healthy employees are nearly three times more productive than those with poor health. A study of nearly 20,000 employees by Brigham Young University, found that employees with unhealthy habits cause substantially higher levels of lost workplace productivity.

Results indicated that employees with healthy eating habits were twenty-five per cent more productive, and those who exercised at least three times a week were fifteen per cent more likely to have better job performance. The overall absenteeism rate for employees who ate healthily and exercised regularly was twenty-seven per cent lower than colleagues who didn't practice these habits.[19]

If you have leadership ambitions and recognise that your health might not be up to the job, perhaps it's time to consider your options, seek medical advice and, if appropriate, create new, healthier routines.

## We are more human

Howard Schultz, the long-time CEO of Starbucks, said, 'Our role as leaders is to celebrate the human connection that we have been able to create as a company'.

Why is being human so important? Mainly because people do business with people they know, love and trust, and a great way to earn trust is to show your human side.

Fiona Brown, CEO of The Society of Consumer Affairs Professionals Australia (SOCAP Australia), told me, 'People don't want robot leaders. Don't try and pretend to be someone different. You don't have to pretend to be more than you are because you have value. I make mistakes – all people do. We are not machines, and that's okay'.

> Our modern workforce is increasingly based on relationships.

It's so important to remember this because our modern workforce is increasingly based on relationships. Disconnected leaders don't understand or value the importance of creating real human connections with their colleagues and others. They operate out of self-interest, demonstrate poor insight and judgement, and have disconnected – if not dysfunctional – teams.

Relationships require a constant give and take. The greater our self-awareness, the greater our knowledge of our quirks and understanding of how others might perceive us, the more flexible this give and take will be.

In her book *Real Communication*,[20] Gabrielle Dolan writes that four qualities make leaders more human.

- They use real language and steer clear of corporate jargon and acronyms.
- They admit mistakes and say sorry when they are wrong. Not a fake sorry, such as, 'I am sorry if what I said caused offence' but rather, 'I am sorry for being offensive'.
- Their personal and professional values are congruent, and they are prepared to take a stand on these.

- They take time to get to know the people they lead and the customers they serve.

Fiona Brown says that showing her true self, especially on platforms such as LinkedIn, has added a lot of value to how SOCAP is seen as an organisation and perceptions of her as a leader. It builds meaningful relationships with SOCAP's members that are essential for the organisation's future.

When we are more human, we also have a greater capacity for developing and strengthening relationships. We do this by showing up with authenticity, vulnerability and empathy.

## *Authenticity*

'The move to more remote work absolutely means you have to bring *more* of yourself to work, right? You can't hide anymore! You're on Zoom, and people can see how you live. There are dogs, there are kids, there's noise. Stuff happens. It's a great opportunity to show our real selves and our real lives. And this makes us more relatable to the people we are working with.' These words are from Kim Stockham, former director of corporate communications at Expedia Group (Asia Pacific).

People who are authentic at work have greater job satisfaction, are more engaged and happier at work, have a stronger sense of community, are more inspired and experience lower job stress.

Two of my women friends had very senior leadership roles in the corporate sector. Both have incredibly curly hair, but for years wore it straight, spending thousands of dollars and hours on treatments and blow-dries to remove the curls. When they realised they could be their true curly-haired selves at work, each said they felt a huge weight lift. It may seem superficial, but inauthenticity can start by denying a simple fact about yourself.

When you are confident to show your real self, your workplace experience can be better. Authenticity also inspires loyalty and engagement, meaning stronger and better relationships with our clients and co-workers.[21]

Mark Anderson is the CEO of Collingwood Football and Netball Club. He says authenticity is an essential quality for leaders. 'If leaders want to have long, or even medium, term success, they need to be themselves and hold true to what they believe. Great leaders are also authentic in their communication. This includes what they stand for, but also their communication style. They need to be truly aligned with who they are as people, in a way that is genuine, as this is crucial for great leadership.'

Mark says that it is always essential for leaders to be vulnerable and open to advice. 'We never have all the answers, so if you're not sure of the right way to communicate, particularly in areas which are sensitive or you don't have a deep level of understanding, don't be afraid to seek out advice or help from an expert.'

## *Vulnerability*

A big part of being human, and a critical part of good leadership, is our willingness to demonstrate our vulnerability.

When we share our vulnerable side, we open ourselves to feelings of shame, weakness, and embarrassment. But vulnerability is so powerful because people can relate to it, and it helps them feel a connection to you.

Vulnerability makes us appear strong and brave.

At work, this shows itself in many ways. It's about not being afraid to say you don't know, owning your mistakes and asking questions. We demonstrate vulnerability when we ask for help, talk about our feelings (especially when they are negative), and in open and honest conversations about our mental health challenges.

In her Netflix special, *The Call to Courage*, Brené Brown says, 'Vulnerability is not about losing, it is about showing up when you can't control the outcome'. She explains that we are hard-wired to care what others think, but we need to be intentional about who we listen to and accept feedback from.[22]

> Vulnerability makes us appear strong and brave.

Entrepreneur and former CEO of software company Moz, Rand Fishkin, knows a lot about vulnerability. His 2014 blog post[23] about his resignation from Moz due to his struggle with depression has long stayed with me, mainly because it was the first time I had read something so raw written by a CEO.

For Fishkin, vulnerability is a sign of power for people within a company. He believes 'When people feel safe being vulnerable in a team environment, they don't have to be individual champions. That [whole] team performs well.'[24]

When we demonstrate vulnerability, we are more relatable and trustworthy because we own how we feel and are prepared to accept the discomfort it can bring.

As Brené Brown says, it means that we choose courage over comfort.

### *Demonstrating empathy*

One of my favourite quotes is from Maya Angelou, who wrote, 'I've learned that people will forget what you said, people will forget what you did, but people will never forget how you made them feel'.

Never underestimate the ability to understand what another person is thinking and feeling and provide relevant support. A few years ago, I was reading a sad book on the train in Brisbane and tweeted the author, saying, 'Damn you, Charlotte, for making me cry on the train. Page 175 of *Love & Hunger* dredged up many memories that are all too recent.' Some ten minutes later, Queensland Rail tweeted me and asked, 'Would you like some tissues?' Fortunately, I had some.

> Choose courage over comfort.

In its Army Field Manual on Leader Development,[25] the United States Army describes empathy as a key characteristic for strengthening relationships and earning trust, particularly from subordinates, since seeing from another's viewpoint helps a leader better understand those around them.

Research by the Center for Creative Leadership found that empathy is positively related to job performance, and managers who show more empathy towards direct reports are viewed as better performers by their superiors.[26]

## We energise our co-workers

When we understand what gives us energy and what saps it, we know what we need to do to recharge our batteries. And when we feel energised and invigorated, we pass these feelings on to the people around us.

'Relational energy' means we 'catch' energy through our interactions with other people. And this impacts our performance at work. Research by Wayne Baker, Bradley Owens, Dana Sumpter and Kim Cameron found that relational energy impacts employee engagement and job performance.[27]

Some people are energising because they give off positive vibes, others because they create genuine connections. For example, they listen to understand when having a conversation. If you are an energising boss, your people are more likely to feel engaged at work, leading to greater productivity.

This research also found that your performance improves when you generate relational energy in the workplace. The more people you energise, the better your performance. This happens because people want to be around you. Your energy also attracts talent, generates new ideas and sparks creativity and innovation.

Ben Vasiliou, CEO of non-profit Youth Projects, believes that connection comes from the energy people give up and the energy he gives off. He says, 'The energy you share when you are in the same room as someone else will tell you far, far more than words through a screen ever will'.

When I asked Ben how he managed his energy to inspire his workforce, he told me that as a leader, there is a certain expectation around the energy that you should be giving off depending on the situation or circumstance. He went on to say that he feels comfortable communicating to his people that his energy may be off for a variety of reasons.

'As a leader and CEO, it's okay not always to be the loudest voice in the room, or even the most energetic person in the room. And it is definitely okay to communicate why you're feeling the way you are. Sharing my vulnerability is important, but so is creating a space for other people to share how they're feeling, and help them understand the impact their energy has on others.'

If you lead a small team or (like me) you work for, and mostly by yourself, consider creating a personal energy group.

About a year ago, my friends Julia and Louisa and I decided to form an accountability group to support each other and stay on track to achieve our goals. We joined forces because we are all at similar places with our work and have similar ambitions. And of course, we like each other. An unexpected benefit is the energy boost from our conversations and daily text messages. I know that my creativity and focus have significantly increased since we joined forces – so much so that they deserve a good chunk of credit for this book.

Conversely, we can also pass on negative energy. If you de-energise others, they won't go out of their way to work with you, buy from you, help you or support you.

My friend Tanya recently resigned from her job – primarily because her boss was an energy vampire. His negativity and total lack of self-awareness ate into her energy so much that she felt she had no other option than to resign. This organisation lost a great leader because her boss couldn't see what a negative impact he was having.

# We communicate with conviction

Richard Branson said, 'Communication is the most important skill any leader can possess'.

Communicating with conviction is the cornerstone of trusted leadership. Our purpose shines through and leaves a lasting impact when we do so. We are unafraid to be authentic, which earns loyalty and trust. We communicate with clarity, confidence, and compassion, motivating, educating, and inspiring.

Conviction creates change, energises individuals and teams, leads to alignment of values and purpose, and achieves greater results.

When we communicate with conviction, we have confidence. We are also more likely to communicate with heart, as we understand and prioritise our people. We demonstrate empathy, compassion, generosity, and a willingness to listen. We keep our ego in check, although ego is like oxygen – we need some to keep the flame alive, but not so much that it creates a raging out-of-control fire.

## Conviction creates change.

Fully connected leaders communicate proactively and strategically rather than constantly reacting to what's happening around them. Yes, it can be hard to find time for deep work and strategic thinking, but it's a critical part of leadership today.

Reactive leaders, driven by ego, can come across as cocky or arrogant. They harm collaboration, innovation and motivation with their strong need to always be right. They are known for changing direction on a whim, have poor listening skills and don't even *try* to tell them what to do.

In his Forbes article *Why the Best Leaders Have Conviction*, Travis Bradberry wrote, 'Leaders with conviction create an environment of certainty for everyone. When a leader is absolutely convinced that he's chosen the best course of action, everyone who follows him unconsciously absorbs this belief and the accompanying emotional state.'[28]

## Leaders who care, communicate

Queensland Country Bank CEO Aaron Newman is the type of leader who tries to be as honest and transparent as possible. He frequently holds all-staff meetings, encouraging his staff to ask him anything. I attended one of these sessions and was struck by his candour. There was only one question he couldn't answer, and that was because the details were confidential to all but a few. Even then, he clearly explained why he couldn't respond and gave a timeframe for providing an update.

Aaron's view is, 'I'll always give my staff as much information as they want, when I legally can. I don't think that attitude exists everywhere, which is a shame because I believe it helps people feel more connected to the business. I understand that not everybody will be completely fascinated with the key strategies of the business because they may not affect their specific position. But I'm keen to help anyone who wants to know, understand what's going on, where we need to make some improvements and why.'

His willingness to share information with clarity, compassion and consistency means he has earned a high level of trust.

This was demonstrated in mid-2020 when, with little certainty about the future of the business due to Covid, he jumped on a video call to ask all staff if they would be willing to postpone their annual pay increase until December. Almost eighty per cent of staff voted in favour of that change.

Aaron believes their agreement was because of his open communication style and his clear explanation of why it was important to the bank.

## The cost of poor communication

One of the greatest benefits of communicating with conviction is that we save our organisations a *lot* of money. Poor communication costs millions – in lost sales and at a fundamental level.

Did you know that, on average, workers waste almost an entire day every week because of inefficient communication and substandard collaboration? And a second day each week is taken up with writing and responding to emails.[29]

Poor communication can lead to:

- staff not understanding their purpose
- pointless meetings that should have been a phone call
- increased reputational risk
- loss of credibility and trust with staff, customers and core stakeholders, resulting in lost sales
- loss of morale and staff feeling unvalued
- reduced innovation
- delayed or failed projects.

And then there is the cost of staff turnover. This goes beyond the obvious costs of recruitment, onboarding and training. Consider the loss of knowledge and the overall productivity and performance of the team, especially if the members worked well together.

Poor communication is often the primary consideration when good people resign. If you see a resignation trend, perhaps look at how your managers and leaders communicate with their people.

Critically, good communication helps avoid the cost of misunderstanding and positively impacts financial performance.

Towers Watson found that companies with highly effective communication practices had forty-seven per cent higher total returns to shareholders over five years (2004-2009) than those with less effective communication.[30]

## We create cultures of belonging

When fully connected to ourselves, we are more likely to feel that we belong, as belongingness is the driving force of human behaviour. Our sense of belonging to a social or work community provides a sense of security that makes our brains happy and helps keep us safe.

> When fully connected to ourselves, we are more likely to feel that we belong.

In a 2021 article in *Harvard Business Review*, Julia Taylor Kennedy and Pooja Jain-Link reported that we are seen for our unique contributions and connected to our co-workers when we belong at work.[31] We are supported in our daily work and career development, and proud of our organisation's values and purpose.

The core benefit of feeling we belong at work is that we become more aligned with purpose and people. Aligned employees lead to better business outcomes. A survey by Corporate Rebels indicated the following consequences:

- absenteeism down by 37%
- accidents reduced by 48%
- 41% of defects eliminated
- productivity up 22%
- profit up 21%.[32]

Our people feel like they belong when they feel valued and cared for.

I once had a manager say, 'I shouldn't need to say "thank you", I pay you.' Let's just say I quit that job soon after *that* enlightening conversation.

Doug Conant is a former president and CEO of Campbell Soup Company. He wrote that you must first win in the workplace to win in the marketplace.

Unsurprisingly, more than eighty per cent of employees say they are motivated to work harder when their boss shows appreciation for their work. Research also links gratitude at work with employees having more positive emotions, less stress, fewer sick days, a greater sense of what can be achieved, more job satisfaction and a greater appreciation for co-workers.[33][34]

When we have a personal gratitude practice, it is more likely to become a regular practice within our teams. Employees feel appreciated and valued, and their productivity and engagement increase by leaps and bounds.

Gratitude at work also leads to feelings of belonging. How often do you say 'Thank you' at work? And how do you show appreciation for the day-to-day work being done? Key milestones are often celebrated, but people need to feel valued and important every day if they are to bring their best to work.

My husband Shaun is a reformed management accountant who now works for a major supermarket delivering people's groceries. There are two things he loves about his job: he is never asked to break the law (seriously, four employers asked him to do this when he was an accountant), and all his customers are happy to see him because he saves them from having to go to the shops, deal with traffic and crowds, then lug the groceries inside.

Shaun's boss also loves him because when she calls at 5am to say, 'Someone hasn't turned up, how quickly can you get here?', he jumps out of bed, gets dressed and heads out the door. I've lost count of how many times his supervisors have given him a box of chocolates and a handwritten thank you card.

It is such a simple gesture, but it makes him feel incredibly valued. It also makes me less irritated by those 5am wake-up calls. #notamorningperson

When you show gratitude to your staff, their job satisfaction increases,[35] and they are willing to go above and beyond what is expected. This satisfaction is passed on to the customer.

Furthermore, organisations must demonstrate that they genuinely care about their people to be competitive in today's workplace. The importance of feeling cared for at work cannot be overstated. Research from Limeade Institute[36] indicates that when employees feel cared for:

- they feel included in their organisation
- they are likely to recommend their organisation as a great place to work
- they feel personally engaged in their work
- they have wellbeing in their life
- they feel their stress is manageable and are not burned out.

This is even more important when considering the rise of loneliness and social isolation, as discussed in Chapter One.

## What resonates?

Does one of the items listed above resonate more than the others?

Do you want to feel happier or healthier? Or do you want to be a bit more human to improve your relationships?

Or are you more interested in the flow-on effects at work?

Keep these in mind as you progress through the book, and we discuss self-awareness, self-motivation and self-care.

# Reflection questions

How are you feeling right now? About your life, your relationships and your work?

_____
_____
_____

What is making you feel this way?

_____
_____
_____

How would you like to feel?

_____
_____
_____

Why do you want to feel this way?

_____
_____
_____

## FULLY CONNECTED

What one or two things can you do today to become more fully connected?

_____

_____

_____

# Part Two

# Prioritise Yourself

Becoming fully connected is not easy, but it's worth it.

Fully connected leaders understand their fears and flaws. They know what they stand for and can motivate and inspire others. They have a healthy approach to life and prioritise their health.

There are three steps to becoming fully connected.

- Become more self-aware: This takes you from being present to having presence. It means having a greater understanding of who you are – your feelings and emotions, attitudes and behaviour, your values, strengths and weaknesses.
- Become more self-motivated and take action: Self-motivated people take responsibility for their lives. They make things happen rather than wait for luck to come their way. It involves knowing your purpose, understanding what gives and saps your energy, and having a leader's mindset.
- Prioritise self-care: Self-care is critical to our mental, emotional and physical health, as it builds resilience. While self-care looks different for everyone, prioritising ourselves demonstrates that we believe we are worthy of being our top priority.

The chapters in Part Two provide practical suggestions and tools to help you work out how you can best prioritise yourself.

# Chapter Three:

# Become More Self-aware

Like too many women, I used to turn down personal and professional opportunities, thinking I wasn't deserving enough, good enough, or experienced enough.

Some twenty years ago, I attended an event at the Queensland University of Technology, where Wendy McCarthy spoke. There were three speakers, and I went to hear the other two, as I hadn't then heard of Wendy.

Her speech changed my life.

Wendy recounted the story of being approached by Senator John Button in 1983. He asked her to consider putting her name forward to become an Australian Broadcasting Corporation board member. She was so astonished by the suggestion that she said 'Yes', while meaning to say 'No'.

It's the next part of her story that I found fascinating.

You can read more about Wendy in her biographies, *Don't Fence Me In*[37] and *Don't Be Too Polite, Girls,*[38] but in 1983, at the age of forty-one, Wendy was already a trailblazer. She became a co-founder of the New South Wales branch of the Women's Electoral Lobby in 1972. She joined the Childbirth Education Association, where she campaigned to allow fathers to be present at the birth and for abortion-law reform. She was executive director of Family Planning Australia; and an inaugural member of the National Women's Advisory Council (NWAC).

Despite all these achievements, Wendy still couldn't work out why she had been approached and was terrified that she would be out of her depth on the ABC board. What could she possibly contribute? How would she compare with the other members? How would she actually *do* this role?

I was mesmerised by her words. How could this smart, influential and inspiring woman feel so undeserving? How could *she* have imposter syndrome?

She ended by saying, 'If someone believes in you enough to give you a huge opportunity, then you owe it to yourself to believe that you can do it. You don't need to say yes to every opportunity, but you do need to consider them. Especially when they seem big and scary.'

Over the following weeks and months, I couldn't get Wendy's words out of my mind. Seriously, after more than twenty years, I still think about them. Whenever my first reaction is no, I stop and question why. Are there valid reasons? Or am I scared because I don't believe I'm good enough or don't have all the right skills?

I don't know what my life would look like today if I hadn't gone to that event all those years ago. But I suspect it would be quite different, thanks to the opportunities I have said yes to when my first inclination was to say no.

When I heard Wendy speak, I was a few months into one of the best jobs I had ever had. I was shocked to get an interview, let alone be offered the job. I said yes because I had just moved to a new city and was unemployed, and the job sounded incredibly exciting. Which it was.

However, not long after starting this role, I began to feel like a complete fraud. I didn't believe I had the experience or the qualifications to do it justice. It wasn't long before I spent a ridiculous amount of time each day wondering why I'd been hired. I imagined my boss, her boss and my colleagues realising I had no idea what I was doing. And, worst of all, I wondered when it would all come crashing down.

My inner critic was in full flight, and my self-awareness was low.

Listening to Wendy speak helped me realise that I *did* deserve this role. I took time to assess my feelings and why I believed I wasn't worthy of the opportunity. I also summoned the courage to ask my boss why she hired me over many seemingly more worthy applicants. Some of whom had made it clear they were very unhappy about my appointment. Gotta love *those* people. My boss's response helped me understand that I did have the skills, the experience and the expertise needed to succeed. She told me she believed in me, and, most importantly, I believed her.

# What's your story?

As humans, we all tell ourselves stories every day.

These stories provide an insight into our subconscious mind – our dreams, our fears, and our desires. They shape our moods, our happiness and our relationships.

Our stories can encompass the good, the bad and the ugly, defining our past, present and future.

We tell ourselves negative stories:

'It's too hard.'

'It needs to be perfect.'

'I'm not good enough.'

'I don't deserve this.'

'If I ignore it, it will go away.'

'I can't take time off work, no one can do the work I do.'

Often our stories are influenced by others. For example, many little (and not so little) girls believe that 'girls can't do maths'. The stories we are told shape the stories we tell ourselves. Acknowledging our stories and understanding their influence is a barometer of our self-awareness.

The power comes when we change the stories from negative to positive. Changing our stories can change our view of the world. This can be life-changing. When we are conscious of our stories, we open our minds to new opportunities and greater self-belief.

What if we flipped those negative stories into positive ones:

'I can do this.'

'Done is better than perfect.'

'Let's give it a go and see what happens.'

'I've worked really hard for this success.'

'Perhaps I should ask some questions about this.'

'I need some time off to recharge, and they will get on fine without me for a while.'

Self-awareness is knowing our personal story. We understand what we stand for and how our upbringing and personal history created who we are today. We see ourselves clearly and objectively and are more aware of how others perceive us.

Self-awareness takes you from being present to having presence.

> **Self-awareness takes you from being present to having presence.**

Many years ago, a friend in the music industry told me about a young artist who was more talented than anyone he had ever worked with. This artist had the opportunity to record in Nashville and the talent and potential to be as big, if not bigger, a star as Keith Urban. Yet this man is not a global household name today because he believed he knew it all. He wouldn't take direction or listen to the experts who wanted the best for his career. He thought he had what it took to achieve international fame and fortune exactly as he was. His fixed mindset, stubbornness and ego blocked him from seeing opportunities, and consequently, he didn't achieve his dream.

A lack of self-awareness is arguably the greatest obstacle leaders face. It can impact personal and professional success, career advancement and how others see you.

What stories do you tell yourself?

What might be holding you back?

Fortunately, we have the power to stop the negative head-talk and respond positively.

In her book *Mindful Relationships*,[39] psychologist Dr B. Grace Bullock suggests the following exercise.

> Take a few moments to write down your personal identity story. Use simple descriptive phrases like, 'I am strong', 'I look after others before myself', 'I am bad with money'. You may also choose to write

down experiences, family beliefs or other influences that helped to shape how you view yourself now.

Once you have listed your beliefs and identified a few of your stories, look at each one and ask yourself the following questions:

- Where did this story come from?
- Is this my story or someone else's?
- Is this story true for me now?
- Is this story contributing to or undermining my happiness?
- Do I choose to continue to live this story, or is it time to write a new one?

Now rewrite your story. When you recognise familiar words, phrases and interpretations of yourself coming to mind (especially the negative ones), acknowledge they are there and rewrite them. Get in the habit of telling yourself your new story over and over again. Instead of, 'I'm not a good person, I don't deserve to be happy', try 'I am wonderful. I deserve all the happiness in the world.'

Bullock says the most effective strategy for working with your personal stories or readjusting your mindset is to observe your thoughts objectively and refrain from getting too attached to them. You need to remember that you are not your story, and your story does not define you. It

**You are not your story.**

is up to you to be aware of these stories and decide whether to live by them.[40]

## The problem with how we perceive ourselves

The stories we tell ourselves shape how we perceive ourselves. And this impacts how we believe other people see us. We judge ourselves based on how we think and feel, but others judge us by our actions and behaviours.

In her book *Insight,* organisational psychologist Tasha Eurich says, 'When we see ourselves clearly, we are more confident and more creative. We make sounder decisions, build stronger relationships, and communicate more effectively. We're less likely to lie, cheat, and steal. We are better workers who get more promotions. And we're more-effective leaders with more-satisfied employees and more-profitable companies.'[41]

My friend Lisa O'Neill puts it rather more succinctly when she says, 'Without awareness, you risk being an asshole!'

I was at a networking event recently, and twice, attendees came and interrupted while I was in the middle of a conversation. Neither of the interrupters noticed or cared that we were talking. They just butted in to talk about themselves. To describe their lack of awareness as frustrating is an understatement. One has since emailed to ask if I could please send him any suitable referrals. Um, no. I don't think so.

Eurich indicates that ninety-five per cent of people think they're self-aware, but the reality is closer to ten or fifteen per cent. 'On a good day, eighty per cent of us are lying to ourselves about whether we're lying to ourselves. It can be problematic. Often, the people who have the most room to improve are the least likely to know.'[42]

Leaders need self-awareness to be effective, as it means you can separate your self-worth from what you do.

Mindset coach Ben Crowe's clients include 2022 Australian Open Tennis winner Ash Barty, surfing queen Stephanie Gilmore and leaders at the World Health Organization. He says, 'When you know who you are and you can own your story ... you don't get distracted by these expectations of others or expectations of the outcome.'

Crowe says one of the main reasons Ash Barty has had such success is because she has an 'extraordinarily clear perspective' of herself, which helps her focus on the task at hand. 'Ash has been on a beautiful journey and done an enormous amount of heavy lifting to work out who she is and find that unconditional sense of self ... realising that tennis is what she does, but it's not who she is.'[43] [44]

Having a solid understanding of our attitudes, behaviours, feelings, values, strengths, and weaknesses means we can see ourselves more clearly. It makes us less likely to fall into the dangerous trap of hubris – also known as believing your own PR. That happens when you start believing everything said about you in introductions and interviews or thinking that you know more than others around the table.

Leaders can have a significant impact on people's lives. Many people will want to be close to you, often for the wrong reasons. They will tell you what you want to hear or what they think you want to hear.

A leader with a strong sense of self knows and understands that their position is merely a role they play at a given moment. Who they are, however, should remain consistent over time.

Jim is a senior executive who believes his leadership skills are exceptional and that he is highly respected within his organisation and more widely across the sector. However, Jim is known for blaming others for his mistakes, taking credit for his team's work and not providing direction when needed. He also responds to bad news with anger, which means his team now sanitises any information he is given.

Jim's perception is that he is a leader extraordinaire. Sadly, his attitude and behaviour are well-known across the organisation, and he is poorly regarded by most of the workforce. Consequently, the culture in his team is dysfunctional, bordering on toxic, and absenteeism and presenteeism are rife.

Compare Jim with Aaron Newman, who I described in Chapter Two.

Aaron believes it is essential for leaders to have a strong sense of self-awareness and demonstrate this in their communication. His staff are encouraged to provide him with feedback to ensure he delivers the right messages at the right time.

## Understanding yourself

Becoming self-aware is all about understanding yourself. The more you know yourself, the greater your self-esteem, self-worth and self-confidence.

It requires a good knowledge of the following aspects of your life.

### Feelings and emotions

One of my favourite movies is Disney's *Inside Out*.[45] It's set in the mind of Riley, an eleven-year-old girl. Her five core feelings, Joy, Sadness, Anger, Fear and Disgust, help her navigate her new life as she and her family move from Minnesota to San Francisco. Joy acts as the leader and, along with Fear, Anger and Disgust, tries to limit Sadness's influence. The overarching message of the movie is that you can't have joy without sadness, because sadness makes joy so much sweeter.

The words 'feelings' and 'emotion' are frequently used interchangeably, but there are differences. Emotions are physiological responses to something, while feelings are our physical and mental reactions as we process the emotion.

For example, if your boss offers to give you some feedback, you might experience the physiological reactions of your heart rate increasing, sweaty palms, and a sick feeling in your stomach. These are emotional reactions that we can't control. The mental reactions of fear, anxiety or worry are feelings.

Brené Brown's research[46] found that most people can only identify three feelings – happy, sad and mad, so it shouldn't be a surprise that most people don't understand their emotions and feelings. And, most of us, even if we do understand them, don't have the tools to manage them.

My friend Catherine Medhurst specialises in leadership and organisational culture, and her purpose in life is to bring exceptional human leadership to organisations. She works with leaders to help them understand how they are showing up – especially those who may have turned down or muted their level of self-awareness.

Catherine sees emotions as data. It's input, not the single source of truth. However, it's valuable information about how you feel and how others will experience you.

One of Catherine's skills is helping leaders see the benefit of valuing emotion as a data source. She does this by getting them to label their emotions and explain how they feel. Then she challenges leaders to question whether this emotion serves and supports how they want to feel and be experienced by others. She likens it to toddlers having a tantrum – they're not happy with the situation, but they haven't got the vocabulary to explain themselves. Your emotions can be a superpower. Name it, tame it and dial up your self-awareness to unlock performance.

> Name it, tame it and dial up your self-awareness.

Fully connected leaders know their emotions and feelings, allow themselves to safely experience a wide range and understand what they need to do to manage them – both at home and at work.

The two emotions most seen in the workplace are anger and stress.

According to Professor Neal Ashkanasy, many leaders fail to acknowledge the importance of emotions in the workplace. 'Conventional wisdom assumes that people leave their feelings at home and are completely rational at work. Nothing could be further from the truth ... and mood management may be one of the most critical elements of leadership.'[47]

Psychologist, Dr Susan David,[48] suggests three ways to understand your emotions better:

- Broaden your emotional vocabulary: Name the emotion (positive or negative) you are currently feeling, and think of two or three other words that also describe it. For example, if you're feeling angry, you might also be frustrated, annoyed or spiteful. If you're feeling happy, other words might be grateful, relieved or excited.

- Think about the intensity of the emotion: There are degrees of anger, stress, joy and happiness. For example, when I'm annoyed, I can be a bit miffed (such as when I find a typo in a newsletter I've already sent out) or incredibly angry (when I find out someone has deceived me), or anything in between. Having insight into the intensity helps you better manage your feelings. How can you rate your emotions on a scale of 1-10? How deep is the emotion you are currently feeling?

- Write out how you feel: When we write down our feelings, we process them better, as the act of writing offers insights into what the feeling meant. Use phrases such as 'I have learned,' 'It struck me that,' 'The reason that,' 'I now realise,' and 'I understand,' to gain a new perspective on your emotions and understand them and their implications more clearly.

We feel many different emotions across a day. These are a few I have felt:

- frustrated because I didn't sleep very well and because it was still raining
- relief when it stopped raining
- happiness when I went out for breakfast

- surprised when my breakfast burrito had chickpeas and not black beans
- grateful that the internet didn't drop out when I ran an online masterclass for a client
- anxious about some impending deadlines
- overwhelmed when I watched the news on TV
- filled with wonder when I saw the sunset.

Had you asked me to describe these a few years ago, I would probably have said happy, sad, annoyed, or grateful.

If you want to better tune in to your emotions, try this exercise:

> At the end of the day, sit down with a pen and paper and write down five or six different feelings you had during the day. Try not to use happy, sad or mad.
>
> Think about how strong each feeling was and rate it, with ten being the most intense and one being the least.
>
> Share at least one of these feelings with someone you love and trust – your partner, a close friend, colleague or family member. It could be as simple as 'I felt joy when I heard my favourite song on the radio' or something deeper and more serious.

Do this a few times a week, and you will soon have a much better understanding of the different emotions you feel.

## Attitude

Your attitude is your predisposition to certain ideas, values, people, systems, and institutions. Frequently they are the result of your experiences, upbringing and education.

Attitudes are shaped by feelings and emotions, linked to our mental state, and help shape behaviour. We will talk further about behaviour in the next section.

Psychologists describe attitudes as:

- Cognitive – how your attitude helps you form thoughts and beliefs.
- Behavioural – how your attitude influences your behaviour.
- Emotional – how you feel about a topic, person, event or object.

Psychologists also describe four types of attitudes, and different circumstances can cause these to change:

Positive attitude: You have a positive mindset – probably a growth mindset – and you assume the best regardless of circumstances. People with a positive attitude look for the good in people and situations. They are happy, confident, energetic and motivated to succeed.

Negative attitude: People with this attitude tend to have a fixed mindset and are inclined to run away from problems. They frequently have little self-awareness and are often angry, doubtful and frustrated with life's experiences. While most of us will have a negative attitude from time to time, it's detrimental personally and professionally if it lasts for too long. A bad attitude is like a flat tyre – you can't go anywhere until you change it.

Neutral attitude: These people tend to ignore what's happening in life and wait for other people to look after them. They are also usually lazy.

Sikken attitude: Avoid these people at all cost. Think of the most toxic and destructive person you know – chances are this describes them.

Dale Carnegie is famous for saying, 'Our mental attitude is the X-factor that determines our fate'. He has also said that 'Happiness doesn't depend on any external conditions; it is governed by our mental attitude'.

The good news is that attitudes are not set in stone; we have control over them. We can choose an attitude of self-compassion, encouragement and motivation, or one of self-sabotage and self-pity. Everyone has bad days and good days. We all experience hurt feelings, grief and physical pain. How do you choose to respond? That is what matters. That is what you can control.

My favourite attitude is gratitude.

If you really set your mind to be grateful, you'll stop paying attention to small annoyances and negative situations.

Instead, you'll start focusing on the good things and the lessons you've learned, even from unpleasant events or encounters.

My friend Emma McQueen shared this on Instagram (@emmarmcqueen) during one of Melbourne's many Covid lockdowns. 'I question if it is happiness or contentment or peace or self-assuredness or all of those things. It actually doesn't matter what the name is, but what I am starting to see is that even on the tough days, you can still choose hope, gratitude and happiness. I think it's about activating my own happiness. It's a nice place to be.'

In his book, *Everyone Communicates, Few Connect*, John C. Maxwell writes, 'People may hear your words, but they feel your attitude'.[49] If you're worried about your attitude and you want to change it, the good news is that you can.

Letting go of a negative attitude is not easy – especially if it's ingrained. And we're quick to slide into negativity when things aren't going according to plan. There have certainly been many times when I've been anxious, stressed or downright angry about situations beyond my control. I'd like to think that I didn't convert this negativity into poor behaviour, but I know that's not always true.

Try doing these things:

> Focus on the positive things in your life. What are you grateful for? A good exercise is to write down three things you're grateful for at the end of each day.

Or buy yourself *The Five-Minute Journal*,[50] which can help you start each day by focusing on the positive.

Stop comparing yourself to others. If you spend a lot of time scrolling through Instagram or Facebook and thinking your life isn't great, stop it. Most people only share the good stuff on social media.

Do random acts of kindness. These can be simple, like holding the door open for someone else, smiling at a stranger, or paying a compliment to a colleague.

Ask for help. Talk to a trusted friend, book in for a session with your work's Employee Assistance Program or see a counsellor.

# Behaviour

The Greek Stoic philosopher Epictetus had it right. It's not what happens to you; it's how you react to it that matters. Behaviour is inextricably linked to attitude.

Your behaviour relates to the action (or inaction) you take to express your attitude and can be verbal or non-verbal.

Bad behaviours can include hostility, anger, dishonesty, disregard for someone else's time, rudeness, bullying, aggression, eye-rolling, and ignoring others. Leaders often neglect accountability. We have all witnessed people not admitting fault when they have clearly done the wrong thing.

Conversely, good behaviours can include kindness, politeness, being civil, being open and honest, compassion, fairness, showing consideration and thoughtfulness, and saying thank you.

A few years ago, I had an experience that made me realise far too many people allow other people's attitudes and behaviours to impact theirs.

We were on holiday in Canberra and, of course, I just happened to park our hire car in one of the only two suburbs impacted by a freak hailstorm. I know. What are the odds? I fronted up to the car rental agency a couple of days later to return the car. The staff, Karen and Ann, were fabulous. They were very apologetic about charging the $4,500 excess (fortunately covered by insurance), but hey, that's their job. No point getting cranky at them.

Suddenly Karen went pale, gasped and looked horrified and mortified as she covered her mouth with both hands. 'Oh no! Oh no! Oh no!' she said.

'What's wrong?'

'I can't tell you. I've made a massive mistake.'

I asked, 'Have you charged me $45,000 by mistake?'.

She went a bit whiter and shook her head, mumbling, 'No, no, no, it's much worse'.

By this time, I was giggling. It turned out that Karen had accidentally charged my credit card with $450,000. I couldn't stop laughing, and Shaun was almost rolling on the floor. This was clearly not the reaction she expected, as she kept repeating, 'Why aren't you angry?'.

I told her it was already done and could easily be fixed by contacting the bank. And that getting angry wasn't going to help anyone, plus, it was funny! I still giggle when I think about it, nearly five years later.

The most shocking part of this experience was that she expected me to be angry, as did her supervisor and colleague. All over a simple mistake that could have happened to any one of us with fat fingers.

I walked away feeling sad that she expected a negative and aggressive reaction that would threaten her and make her feel even worse than she so obviously already did. It spoke volumes about the behaviours of customers she must deal with and how they had impacted her attitude. It also reminded me that when it comes to situations out of our control, we just need to just Let. It. Go. and relax. Sometimes after taking a very deep breath.

Oh, and if you're wondering, of course, the bank didn't let a $450,000 charge go through on a card with only a $10k limit. Sheesh!

My mother used to say, 'You can tell a lot about a person by how they treat the people who serve them'. I paid a lot of attention to this when I was single and dating. On a first date, one guy was highly dismissive of the waitress. He didn't say please or thank you while ordering or when his meal was served. When it came time to leave, he stood and clicked his fingers to get her attention so she would bring over the bill. I was horribly embarrassed and wanted to slink out the back door. Needless to say, there wasn't a second date.

Think about how you treat the people who serve you – the waitstaff in your favourite café, the front desk clerk when you check into a hotel, the checkout person at your supermarket, the flight attendant who serves you a drink. And now think about how you treat them when things aren't going smoothly.

> Our response speaks volumes about character.

People are human, and we make mistakes. When things go wrong, our response speaks volumes about character.

Behaviour change is hard. You need to be aware of what you want to change and be willing to make an effort. With a high level of self-awareness, we are more aware of our behaviour and its impact on others.

There are three things you can do to become more aware of your behaviour:

- Observe your behaviour, particularly when things aren't going well. Are you happy with how you

reacted or responded? What could you have done differently?
- Ask your friends and colleagues when they believe you don't behave appropriately. The willingness to have this conversation says a lot about your desire to change.
- Be kind to yourself.

# Values

Our values are the fundamental qualities and beliefs that drive us and serve as a guide for our behaviour. They are the foundation of our lives and help us determine our priorities. Each of us has a hierarchy of values from most to least important.

When you live according to your values, you are more likely to be living the life you want. Things feel wrong when you make decisions that don't align with your values, leading to discontent and unhappiness.

Make a conscious effort to identify your values. If you're unsure of what they are, try the following exercise:

> Read through the list of the most common values on page 92. Circle the values that resonate with you. Add extra words if some are missing.
>
> Next, start at the top of the list and highlight the eight to ten values that are the most important.

Finally, reread the list and place an asterisk* next to those values you aspire to have and best reflect the person you want to become.

Don't overthink or spend too much time on this exercise. You will instinctively know which values feel right.

How we order these determines our priorities, which dictates how we spend our time. For example, do you choose to spend time at work or get home in time for dinner with your family? Do you sleep in or do some exercise or meditation? Do you stay up late watching Netflix or go to bed early enough to get eight hours of sleep? Do you accept a job with a long commute for more money or a shorter commute for less money? Do you volunteer in your community?

Your values tend to stay the same, but your priorities around them might change.

I suspect you had very different priorities in your twenties compared with the following decades.

One of my values is security – in particular, financial security. That means that in my twenties, my career was my top priority. When I was thirty, I moved from Sydney to Brisbane because I wanted to buy a house, meet a life partner and have a less hectic life. All these things happened because I made them a priority.

At thirty-one, my biggest priority was to save enough money for a house deposit. Now in my fifties, I own my home and am thinking more about financial security for my retirement. How long do I want to work? How much money will I need? What do I need to do to get that?

Life is far easier when your personal values align with your workplace. It can be very challenging when they conflict.

My ex-accountant husband Shaun has high standards about 'doing what's right'. His core values include loyalty, honesty and fairness. When past employers wanted him to do dodgy things with money – things that were highly unethical and bordering on illegal, his values collided, causing significant stress. He resigned and now works for an organisation with similar values to his.

Research from Deloitte[51] shows that millennials, who now make up half the workforce, want to work for executives with a clear vision of how they will help improve society. They make decisions about who they work for, who they buy from and who they volunteer with based on shared values with the organisation. Great, you might think. I can do that.

Unfortunately for most CEOs, seventy-five per cent of these millennials believe that businesses and their leaders have no focus beyond their own narrow agendas.

Oh.

That's probably because most millennials get their news from digital sources. And too few leaders have a presence there. (And yes, I can help you with that!)

**Core values list**

| | | |
|---|---|---|
| Abundance | Freedom | Peace |
| Achievement | Friendship | Perfection |
| Adventure | Fun | Philanthropy |
| Affluence | Gratitude | Pleasure |
| Authenticity | Growth | Poise |
| Authority | Happiness | Popularity |
| Autonomy | Health | Power |
| Balance | Honesty | Recognition |
| Beauty | Hope | Religion |
| Belonging | Humour | Reputation |
| Boldness | Inclusivity | Respect |
| Challenge | Influence | Responsibility |
| Citizenship | Inner harmony | Security |
| Community | Joy | Self-respect |
| Compassion | Justice | Service |
| Competency | Kindness | Spirituality |
| Contribution | Knowledge | Stability |
| Courage | Leadership | Status |
| Creativity | Learning | Success |
| Curiosity | Love | Taking charge |
| Dependability | Loyalty | Tradition |
| Determination | Meaningful work | Trustworthiness |
| Fairness | Moderation | Truthfulness |
| Faith | Money | Wealth |
| Fame | Openness | Wisdom |
| Family | Optimism | |

## Strengths and weaknesses

Our strengths come easily, while our weaknesses don't. Knowing both means understanding how we function best.

When we recognise and focus on our strengths, we are more likely to have the momentum to act. We achieve the results we seek, are more engaged and have greater enjoyment in our personal and professional lives.

Identifying weaknesses allows us to improve and develop, as they can hold us back from achieving success, especially if we are unaware of them.

There are several ways to identify both strengths and weaknesses.

We can ask other people – our friends, supervisors at work, colleagues, and family. A couple of years ago, I asked on Facebook, 'What do you think my biggest skills and strengths are?' Some of the answers were surprising, although most people suggested similar themes – connecting people, communication, and cooking.

Another way to find out is to utilise profiling tools such as the CliftonStrengths Assessment,[52] Enneagram Personality Type Test[53] or the Kolbe Index Assessment.[54] Each of these will provide you with an assessment of your strengths. Knowing your strengths means you can decide to do things that make you shine. It allows you to make smarter choices about your career, goals and overall life. You can spend more time focusing on areas that you're good at and delegate or

> Focusing on our strengths makes us more confident.

outsource the tasks you're not great at.

Focusing on our strengths makes us more confident and more likely to identify opportunities.

While it's important to understand weaknesses, emphasising them can be discouraging and demoralising.

## Improving your self-awareness

Improving self-awareness doesn't magically happen overnight. It takes time and some effort. Things we can do include:

- create space and time for self-reflection
- practice mindfulness
- listen to understand
- be actively curious.

Let's look at each in turn.

## Create space and time for self-reflection

One of our chickens used to hide out in the laying box to get a quiet and safe space away from the others. It was her way of creating space. I don't know what her little chicken brain was thinking, but it was a good reminder that we also should take regular time out for some self-reflection.

Creating time and space for self-reflection is one of the best ways to slow down, shift your mindset, process and challenge your thoughts and feelings, and become more positive.

A study of UK commuters discovered that those who used their commute to think about and plan for their day were happier, more focused, and less burned out than people who didn't.[55] I know that when I used to walk home from work, rather than catch the bus, I felt a lot less stressed as I had time alone to process everything that had happened that day.

If you want to reflect more regularly, you may need to make it a priority. One way to do this is to schedule this time in your calendar. Experiment with the timing – you might want to take time every day, once a week, or once a month. If this is a new practice, you might like to start with ten-fifteen minutes once a week. My friend Sam has two hours a week scheduled in her diary for quiet reflection. This time is sacred, and very few people are allowed to override it. In contrast, my friend Leanne takes fifteen minutes at the end of each workday immediately before shutting down her computer.

Once you have found the time, find the location that works best for you – it's unlikely to be your office. It might be a café, or perhaps a walk or use your commute.

You will probably also want to experiment with the structure. You might write down whatever comes into your mind, or you might prefer to have a set of questions to go through. A few starting questions might be: What worked? What didn't work? What brought me joy today? What frustrated me today?

## Practice mindfulness

Mindfulness is about being in the moment. Being present.

A mindfulness practice doesn't need to include meditation or yoga; however, it does need something that allows you to remove the stress from your life, even if it's for a few moments.

We have 40-80,000 thoughts, and we make 30,000 decisions a day – the cognitive load on our minds is immense. That's why Barack Obama only wore a blue or a grey suit every day and why Steve Jobs always wore jeans and a black turtleneck. It reduces decision fatigue and is why many people have the same thing for breakfast or a regular morning routine.

Taking time to be in the moment reduces our stress, helps control anxiety, reduces chronic pain, and improves sleep. It also opens our minds to new ideas.

Personally, my favourite forms of mindfulness are baking or walking alone, with nothing plugged into my ears.

You might like to try yoga or meditation. Research shows that five minutes of meditation a day changes your brain, and ten minutes boosts creativity.[56]

Or you might like to start a gratitude practice where you reflect on what you are grateful for each day.

Start small if you want to incorporate a daily mindfulness practice but are unsure how to find the time. Some apps offer five-minute meditations. You could journal for five minutes or even sit quietly and focus on your breathing for a few minutes a couple of times a day.

## Listen to understand

Great leaders lead by listening first and asking later. They also listen without judgement.

Listening is a skill we all *think* we have, but most of us are just waiting for our turn to talk. Fully connected leaders listen to understand and then decide whether they have anything of value to add before allowing words to escape their lips.

Not listening can seriously damage relationships. Oscar Trimboli wrote in *Deep Listening* that when we don't listen, people feel undervalued or offended. Not listening also can lead to misunderstandings, feelings of frustration, isolation and increased fear.[57]

**The ability to listen is sexy.**

The ability to listen is sexy. You'll know this if you've ever been on a date with someone who asks the same question repeatedly because *they weren't listening to your answer.* (I'm *sooooo* tempted to name a few of my bad first dates ...)

It's very easy to be distracted (and smartphones are partly responsible here), so focused listening is more essential than ever.

Over time, the ability to truly listen has increased in importance. So many messages compete for our attention, thanks to the bombardment of marketing messages we receive online and offline. In the 1970s, the average consumer saw around five hundred ads per day. Today, it's more like five thousand and increasing.[58]

Our workplaces are filled with distractions. How often have you been in a meeting, and your mind has wandered? Or you've had a sneaky under-the-desk check of your phone and been distracted by an email or text?

What is the impact on people around you if you are not listening? Let's flip it: how do you feel when people don't listen to you? Frustrated? Annoyed? Unvalued? Angry?

If you *really* want to become a better listener, then listen to learn – and not just to be polite. Show curiosity about what and who you are listening to. Ask questions to help you better understand and have an open mind rather than making assumptions.

The key to being a good listener is to focus on the other person – don't be distracted by your phone, email or your next meeting. And know when to leave the conversation – or, perhaps don't even start it. If you've run out of energy or aren't in the right state of mind to listen, then explain to the other person and offer another time when your attention can be more focused. They will appreciate your honesty and commitment to talking with them when you do have time.

## Be actively curious

Albert Einstein famously encouraged us to 'question everything'.

And anyone who has spent time with a young child will know of their insatiable curiosity. Children ask hundreds of questions a day – often starting with 'Why?'.

When do we stop being curious? Is it when we suddenly have to sit in a classroom for six hours a day? Is it when we become too busy with the day-to-day aspects of life? Is it when we discover social media and spend much of our time scrolling mindlessly through Instagram?

Whatever the reason, it's not too late to reinstall curiosity into your life. When we are actively curious, we are interested in finding answers, and we are more open to new ideas and new ways of doing things.

Francesca Gino suggests that when our curiosity is triggered, we think more deeply and rationally about decisions and develop more creative solutions. We have improved decision-making because we are less susceptible to stereotypes and confirmation bias.[59]

> **Curiosity leads to change.**

Curiosity leads to change. It increases our awareness of what is influencing our attitudes, behaviour and feelings, so we can find different ways to take action.

There are so many ways we can increase our curiosity. We can ask more questions – including 'How could we do this differently?' We can listen without judgement and avoid assumptions.

How often do you genuinely observe what's around you? And seek to discover new things? When was the last time you went to an art gallery, travelled a different way to work, read a book or watched a TV show or movie in a genre you wouldn't usually try?

And how often are you curious about yourself? Do you question your beliefs? When was the last time you asked for feedback at work – from a superior or a subordinate – so you could learn and grow?

Curiosity doesn't just happen. Ask yourself how you could become more curious today.

# Self-awareness checklist

- ☐ I have put some time in my schedule for self-reflection
- ☐ Two words that describe how I am feeling right now are _____ and _____
- ☐ Today I am grateful for _____
- ☐ My intention for today is _____
  _____

- ☐ Something I can get excited about today is _____
  _____

- ☐ An act of kindness I could do today is _____
  _____

- ☐ Today I will observe my behaviour when things don't go according to plan
- ☐ I will spend at least five minutes today practising mindfulness
- ☐ I will listen to understand, and I will start by giving the other person my full attention
- ☐ I will seek to be more curious

A printable version of this checklist is available at www.melkettle.com/fullyconnected

# Reflection questions

What are the stories about your life you tell yourself?

_____

_____

_____

What might be holding you back?

_____

_____

_____

How do you perceive yourself?

_____

_____

_____

How do other people – your boss, colleagues, and family – see you?

_____

_____

_____

How would you describe your attitude, and how is this reflected in your behaviour?

_____

_____

What are your top five values?

_____

_____

What are your top three strengths?

_____

_____

How might you focus more on your strengths?

_____

_____

_____

# Chapter Four

# Become Self-motivated and Take Action

During high school, I was desperate to be a Rotary exchange student and live overseas for a year. We had hosted several exchange students in our home, and I was fascinated by their lives, the cultures they grew up in, and their independence from a young age. I also had the travel bug and thought that being an exchange student would be a great way to experience life as a young adult.

My parents were entirely on board with my plan and supported my application through the Rotary Club, where my dad was a member.

There was only one problem – I was excruciatingly shy, and this shyness saw my application rejected.

Fortunately, the guy who was initially selected withdrew, so I got a second chance. A very kind member of the selection committee told me, 'We are putting you forward, but you need to know that we didn't select you initially because you came across as incredibly quiet and shy. And we don't know whether you will fit in.'

I knew that to make the most of this second chance, I would have to push myself out of my comfort zone. I wanted the selectors to see that I would be a great representative for Rotary International, the district, my sponsor club, and, most importantly, Australia.

No pressure.

Mum drove me from Gosford to Sydney for the full-day interview, which was a mix of panel interviews, a group interview, and a lot of time sitting around with the other applicants, parents and Rotarians. I quickly realised that sitting around was the most important part, as this was where our ability to connect and engage was measured. If we couldn't instigate and carry a conversation with our peers and their families, how could we be expected to do so with strangers from other countries and cultures?

> Motivation is the driving force behind getting things done.

Apparently I impressed the selectors because I was accepted, and on 14 January 1988, I flew to Brandon, Manitoba in Canada, for one of the most incredible years of my life. For the first time, I realised that if I truly wanted something, I had to believe in myself and take action to achieve my goal.

Motivation is the driving force behind getting things done. It's what gets us out of bed in the morning and helps us achieve our goals. It can sometimes be tricky to find, which is when we take a step back to understand our core purpose and priorities, find the discipline and create habits that lead to progress.

Self-motivated leaders understand their purpose and priorities, are focused and know what they must do to reach their goals. They encourage themselves to continue taking action, even when it feels challenging.

## Intrinsic or extrinsic?

Humans are motivated by various reasons and guided by factors including individual personality, life experiences, education, culture and upbringing.

Some of us are motivated by reasons that might be considered to be egotistical and selfish, while others are more generous and pragmatic. People whose sole motivation is egotistical or selfish don't usually do well.

Once our fundamental biological drivers of food, water and sexual gratification are met, we can categorise our motivations as intrinsic and extrinsic.

Intrinsic motivation occurs when we do something because we love it or because it challenges us, or because we are curious. I'm motivated to read fiction and prioritise time to do so because I love where the stories take me in my imagination. It's an understatement to say I'm disappointed when a book I love is turned into a movie, and the wrong actors are cast.

Extrinsic motivation occurs when rewards such as money, praise or fame are used as motivation. This reward-led behaviour is driven by external factors. Extrinsic motivation can start from a young age when we are 'rewarded' with dessert for eating our veggies. Or given extra pocket money for 'helping' with chores around the home that really should be done because you're a part of the family. If you do X, we will give you Y.

Examining your motivations to be a leader offers insight into your leadership style.

In her book *On Becoming a Woman Leader*,[60] Susan Madsen writes about the motivations of the ten women university presidents she interviewed. The top reasons they had for leading were:

- to accomplish and achieve
- to make a difference, contribution, or impact
- to be involved in meaningful and important work
- to have challenges and complexity
- to have fun and enjoyment
- to do work that they knew they could do
- to enable others to develop and succeed

- to have power and influence
- to serve.

Interestingly, none of these reasons included money. And even those who said they enjoyed the power and influence tempered their words by saying, 'I like the power to make things happen for others', and 'I believe that power can be useful in serving others and moving efforts along that can truly make a difference.' They liked that having power provided them with the ability to influence, make changes and serve others.

One woman I admire is Sara Blakely, the founder of Spanx and the youngest self-made female billionaire in history. In an interview on the podcast *How I Built This*,[61] she tells host Guy Raz that she didn't create Spanx for the money and that it wasn't something she focused on.

'After a couple of years of Spanx, I was still in my apartment. And my accountant kept trying to convince me to buy a house, and I was like, I don't know, I'm not interested.'

> Knowing your motivation impacts your decisions and choices.

She went on to say that her little brother was always calling and telling her different ways to spend her money, but she wasn't interested. While it was important for her, as a woman, to be able to pay her rent and stand on her own two feet, she just loved making the product and selling it to other women so they could feel better about themselves.

Knowing your motivation impacts your decisions and choices.

Blakely said that in the early days of Spanx, she was often asked about her exit strategy. Because she had never taken a business class, she didn't know what they were talking about – until it dawned on her 'that people actually start things just to sell them'. She said she was always so connected to the product that she was creating it before it happened. She knew she didn't have the most money, a business degree or any real idea of what she was doing in manufacturing or retail, but she cared the most. And she believed in herself. And that belief, along with a lot of determination and persistence, is what led to her success.

# Motivation is nothing without action

Self-motivated people take responsibility for their lives – they make things happen rather than sitting around waiting. They make decisions and back themselves. That isn't to say they don't have self-doubt or fear of failure, but they know how to move through the fear to pursue what's important.

A core part of the ability to make things happen is taking action. And this can be really hard.

Motivated leaders ask themselves, 'What do I want?' and 'Why do I want it?'

Successful leaders ask, 'What do I need to *do* to get what I want?'

Wanting something and doing what is required to get it are two very different things.

Motivation can be flighty; it's discipline that makes you show up every day and do the work, even when you don't want to.

I'm motivated to write this book. But motivation isn't enough for me to sit down every day and work on it. That takes action and a lot of discipline.

Motivation sets the goal, but discipline achieves it.

So how do we find discipline? What do we need to do to take the necessary action to achieve our goals?

I have a couple of mantras. 'Take imperfect action' and 'Done is better than perfect'.

> Motivation sets the goal, but discipline achieves it.

The version of this book you will read is at least #97 (I stopped counting a long time ago). The first version was definitely an example of done being better than perfect. Or, as Anne Lamott described in *Bird by Bird*,[62] it was a shitty first draft. You can work with a first draft. You can't work with a blank page.

Some people find it far easier to take action than others. Perhaps you know someone who is a *gunna* and not a *doer*. Or maybe it's you? Do you find yourself saying, 'I'm going to do this...' but never do?

Before establishing my own practice, I worked for the Queensland State Government for about five years. Like all workplaces, there were pros and cons. I had some fantastic experiences, learned a lot, and met smart, interesting people – some of whom will be lifelong friends.

However, by the five-year mark, I was doing a job I didn't enjoy. I was in a senior role, which meant I was spending most of my time managing people and trying not to get embroiled in the politics (internally and externally). My search for a new role with less people management and similar money was proving fruitless.

I decided it was time to stop being an employee and start working for myself. I was highly motivated to quit my job, but three things stood in the way. The enormous size of our mortgage, Shaun was a contractor with no job security, and I had no idea how to be a consultant, and no clients lined up.

I needed a plan. And I needed to take action.

Shaun and I agreed that before I could quit, I needed to generate enough work to cover the mortgage repayments for at least three months. He needed to get a permanent job, and I needed to apply for – and get – leave without pay for six months, so if everything went pear-shaped, I had a job to go back to. I can tell you now that my biggest incentive to succeed was the threat of having to go back to that job.

So I took immediate action to fill in the paperwork for leave without pay and started the client-finding process. Somewhat freakishly, within three days of our conversation, Shaun was offered a permanent job, I signed up my first client with a large, juicy project, and my leave application was approved. I left, formally resigned at the end of that six months, and I still love being self-employed sixteen years later.

Taking action and having the discipline to achieve your goals can be hard – especially when motivation has left you. Which it is likely to do when the work needs to happen.

# Become an action taker

You can do six things to become more of an action taker.

## 1. Just start

One of my mentors says action begets action. She means that once you start something, you start to build momentum, you get into a routine, and good things happen. If there is something you really want to achieve, just start.

> 'Perfection is the enemy of progress'.

My friend Callum knows that sales calls are a necessary part of his business, but he finds them awkward to make as he doesn't like talking on the phone. Every day when he sits down to make his daily allotment of calls, his first call is to a friend. This quick, two-minute call gets him in the groove, and he is then comfortable enough to call everyone else on his list.

I like to take imperfect action. Rather than overthink something (which I do extremely well), I now just try to start. Remember Winston Churchill's words, 'Perfection is the enemy of progress'.

## 2. Map out a plan

My love of planning can be traced back to my event management days when we reverse-engineered all our conferences. That meant we knew our goal (a successful conference on X date) and worked backwards to unpack what needed to be done and by when.

Today I have a three-year strategy for my practice, chunked into ninety-day action plans.

I love the ninety-day concept as it's enough time to achieve something tangible and work out whether it is likely to succeed. I even used the ninety-day plan when I was single and looking for love (yes, my friends thought I was a bit mad!). My view was that if I spent a few hours each week with the man I was dating, I should know by about the ninety-day mark whether or not I wanted to continue seeing him. Of course, I often knew far earlier, but the timeline was a good indicator of whether we had some sort of future.

To use this concept in my work, I sit down at the end of each quarter and map out what I need to do over the next ninety days to drive me toward my three-year goals. I look at everything – client and personal commitments, anticipated commitments, holidays, long weekends, etc. Then I work out what can I achieve with the time that's left. Next, I work out what I need to do each day and week to achieve my goals. I review it regularly and tweak it where necessary.

## 3. Create the right habits and routines

Having an embedded set of habits and routines means we are more organised and can save time. It can also help us achieve better outcomes, reduce anxiety, have greater confidence and improve performance.

Charles Duhigg is the author of *The Power of Habit*.[63] He writes that a habit is a choice that we deliberately make at some point. We then stop thinking about it but continue doing it, often every day. In other words, a habit is a formula our brains follow automatically. When I see X (cue), I will do Y (routine) in order to get Z (a reward).

Whether simple or complex, every habit has the same habit loop structure. When repeated often enough, you do it automatically, with little conscious thought. At that point, not doing it feels uncomfortable.

One of my daily habits is to clean my teeth before going to bed. The *cue* is that I am about to climb into bed, the *routine* is that I clean my teeth, and the *reward* is that my teeth don't feel fuzzy.

You might have a habit that includes setting your intention for the day, reading, journaling, a gratitude habit, regular exercise, or meditation.

A routine is a behaviour or a set of behaviours that we frequently repeat. Unlike a habit, we can skip or change a routine and not feel awkward about it.

Many fully connected leaders have a morning routine that sets them up for the day. It might include exercise, meditation, family time, breakfast, a cup of tea, watching or listening to the news, or perhaps doing the day's Wordle.

Author and podcaster Tim Ferriss says having a morning routine can help you win the day. If you accomplish one good thing in your morning routine, you're much more likely to have a good rest of the day.[64]

The time interval of your routine can be daily – perhaps it's how you spend the first and last thirty minutes of your workday. It could be weekly, such as setting aside regular thinking and planning time. Or it could be quarterly, such as a long weekend away or reviewing your ninety-day plan.

> Habits and routines remove decisions.

Perhaps the greatest benefit is that habits and routines remove decisions, saving time and reducing overwhelm.

If you want to create a new habit or routine, start simple and start small. Pick one thing you want to start doing and create a habit loop around it. For example, if you want to start meditating, don't immediately plan to do so for thirty minutes a day. That's too hard, so start with five minutes and work your way up to a pace you can sustain.

Don't do as I did a few years ago when I publicly committed to a new morning routine which took two hours a day and included exercise, eating a good breakfast, journaling and reading non-fiction. A few early flights in the first week meant I failed spectacularly.

The only new morning habit I've instilled lately is doing the daily Wordle while drinking my second cup of tea.

## 4. Be ruthless about distractions

My favourite book a few years ago was Nir Eyal's *Indistractible*.[65] The premise is that if we aren't interested in what we are doing, we will always find a way to be distracted. Many people say social media is a huge distraction, and it can be, but if you love what you're doing, you won't be randomly scrolling through Instagram.

And let's face it, people have always found ways to distract themselves from what they should be doing if they don't want to be doing it.

Distractions can get out of hand, so we need to find reasons to focus and set ourselves up for success.

Eyal suggests four strategies:

- Master internal triggers. Understand that most distractions begin from within and are due to uncomfortable feelings like anxiety, stress, and overwhelm. Work out what you need to do to cope with these feelings in a healthy way.
- Make time for traction. Plan your day, so you have control over it. I'm a fan of the idea that things are unlikely to happen unless they are in my calendar. If someone else manages your work calendar (for example, your assistant), then talk about what you want it to look like so you can have time for the important work. Can you block out time, so you're not always in meetings?
- Hack back external triggers. Start by turning *off* the notifications on your devices. Remove apps that aren't necessary or that you can use on your computer and put your phone into greyscale. A massive amount of stress and overwhelm disappeared from my life when I took Facebook and

email off my phone. Give it a go for a few days and see if it makes a difference for you. Even removing email on weekends and holidays can make a positive difference.
- Prevent distraction with pacts. Make precommitments by removing future choices to prevent distractions. Try an app to limit how much time you can spend on social media or talk regularly with an accountability buddy to hold you on track with your goal.

## 5. Track your progress

I'm a big list-maker. Ticking off something I've done gives me a huge dopamine hit. A great way to stay motivated is to measure and track what you have achieved, so you feel good about what you're doing. Researchers Teresa Amabile and Steven J. Kramer found that out of all the things that can boost our mood and keep us motivated during the workday, 'the single most important is making progress on meaningful work'[66].

Here are a few ways to track your progress:

- Break your goal into smaller tasks and set some metrics around them.
- Monitor your progress frequently. As one of my ninety-day actions is to make one hundred sales calls, I have a piece of paper with checkboxes and lines so I can tick the box and write the name of the person I called.

- Have a weekly and a monthly review to identify what you have completed and what you will do next.

Business Chicks Global CEO Emma Isaacs tracks her progress by checking her business cash position each day. Knowing your numbers is an excellent way to track progress, especially if you are responsible for budgets, are a business owner or have financial goals.

You might also want to do what my friend Lisa does. She has weekly meetings with herself to track her progress with some of her life and work goals. Every Monday morning, she takes herself and her notebook out to a café for a coffee and a slice of cake, and spends ninety minutes evaluating her past week and setting some goals for the current week. Each of these relates to her ninety-day plan and her bigger picture ambitions.

## 6. Celebrate the wins

We often celebrate our big wins – major milestones and achieving important goals, but it's easy to get caught up in the day-to-day of work and life and forget to celebrate the small wins.

In his book, *Get Inspiration*, my friend Warwick Merry wrote, 'When celebrating success becomes a habit, success becomes a habit'.[67]

Psychologist and author of *Tiny Habits*, BJ Fogg, says that celebrating is a great way to reinforce small changes and pave the way for big successes.[68] It could be as simple as doing a happy dance every time you have a small win, or something more significant, like buying yourself something you have wanted for a while when you have a big win. For many years, I celebrated gaining a new client by adding a new cookbook to my collection.

When Margot Robbie was promoting the movie *Once Upon a Time in Hollywood*, she said one of the reasons she loved working with director Quentin Tarantino was because he acknowledged the small wins and the big milestones. Quentin responded that we all do this job every day, so we should make sure we enjoy it and have fun.

If you use the ninety-day plan model, could you build in a few celebrations? Think about how you could break large goals into smaller goals, create small milestones and reward yourself.

# Success isn't luck

The American actor Denzel Washington said that luck is when an opportunity comes along, and you're prepared. Far too often, successful people are considered 'lucky'. I'm here to tell you that most lucky people have worked hard for that luck.

When studying for my Master of Public Health degree, I learned that the only time in our life we are truly lucky is if we are born into ideal circumstances, with healthy, loving and financially secure parents, in a country free from conflict, etc. (Okay, so in recent months I've learned that guessing Wordle on your first go is also lucky – a feat I have yet to achieve.)

To help us understand this concept of luck, we played a character-based board game called *The Last Straw*,[69] where each player develops a profile that includes their gender, socio-economic status and race. As you play the game, you move through life stages from childhood to adolescence, adulthood, and old age. At each stage, you encounter 'macro' issues, such as political climate, economic structure and environmental change, and 'micro' issues, such as individual finances, education, and family dynamics. Each player gains or loses vitality chips based on the scenarios. This game was an enlightening way to learn about white male privilege.

Author Margie Warrell tells us to create our own luck. 'Don't wait to feel brave before you start acting as though you were.' She says nothing worthwhile is ever created without risk. 'Push yourself outside your comfort zone and lay your vulnerability on the line for something more important than your pride and short-term safety.'[70]

While luck is a mix of being observant, grabbing opportunities, taking action and being optimistic, British psychology professor Richard Wiseman says that luck can play a role in our lives. In his book *The Luck Factor*[71], he describes how 'lucky' people engage in more eye contact and smile more often. They meet more people, are less neurotic and anxious, and are open to new experiences. He believes that to increase your luck, it's important to:

- Keep an open mind and seek out opportunities.
- Look at the positive side of life and be grateful that bad things weren't worse.
- Listen to your intuition and gut instinct.
- Step outside your comfort zone and do something new or different each week.

I bought my first house, on my own, when I was thirty-two. It didn't take long for many people to tell me how lucky I was. Yet only about one per cent of this was due to luck. If that.

One of the two main reasons I moved to Brisbane at age thirty was because I wanted to buy a house. There was no way I could do that in Sydney, not on my then $50,000 annual income.

In 2000, the residential property market in Brisbane was starting to boom. While I was keen to own, I wasn't quite mentally ready. And I certainly wasn't financially prepared. I moved to Brisbane with a small amount of savings and no job. No way was a bank going to lend me money for a mortgage. By early 2001 I could see that I would be priced out of the market if I didn't get a wriggle on. However, my savings account needed a huge boost, so I decided it was time to make a plan and put it into action. My plan had three components:

1. Get a permanent job so a bank would give me a mortgage. (This happened surprisingly quickly.)
2. Save at least another $20,000 for a deposit. I did this by getting my employer to put fifty per cent of my take-home pay into a separate bank account that was more difficult to access. Living on half my income was hard but doable as I was prepared to make the necessary sacrifices. It meant that for fourteen months, I rarely spent money on handbags, shoes or going out. Basically, nothing other than the essentials. I know. I'm proud of myself too.
3. Start looking at real estate to make an informed choice about where and what to buy once I was ready.

Once the time came, and I had a mortgage pre-approved, I started looking at houses every weekend. It took me six long and often disheartening months to find the right one. Friends told me buying a house was like falling in love – you know immediately. That was certainly true for me. A few hours after walking into the house that I knew *had* to be mine, I made an offer. Thankfully it was accepted three nerve-wracking days later.

So if you want to be lucky, what do you need to do?

To start, lay the groundwork. Know what you want to achieve, set some goals and create a plan. Then you need to execute the plan, while looking out for opportunities, following your instincts, making informed decisions and celebrating success.

## Be clear on your purpose

When we understand our purpose, we are more engaged and motivated at work and in life. Good leaders know their purpose and their employees' purpose and seek to connect them with the organisational goals.

Understanding your purpose drives the decisions and choices you make. It's what will help keep you going when things are hard.

When you know your purpose, it's easier to plan, set goals and then take relevant action to achieve them. When my goals are connected to my purpose, I'm far more likely to achieve them.

> Understanding your purpose drives the decisions and choices you make.

Your purpose distinguishes you from other people – it's like your DNA – it's specific to you. What would happen, or who would care if you ceased to exist?

It's easy to say that you should know your purpose, but not everyone does.

I'm a huge fan of the late Stephen Covey, author of *The 7 Habits of Highly Effective People*,[72] particularly his second habit to 'begin with the end in mind'. I undertook training on this more than twenty years ago, and it still forms the basis of most of my work. However, I have recently started to think about it from a personal perspective, and it can be difficult to answer.

Another proponent of finding your purpose is Simon Sinek. The core of his well-known golden circle is to start with 'Why'.[73] According to Sinek, when we know our why (our purpose), we are more capable of pursuing the things that give us fulfilment. Purpose serves as a reference point for all our actions and decisions. It allows us to measure progress and helps us know when we have achieved our goals.

Few people can clearly articulate their why. It seems like a simple concept, but once you start to think about it, you'll realise it's a bit tricky!

Three good questions to start with are:

1. Why do I get up in the morning?
2. Why should anyone else care?
3. What keeps me awake at night?

Why is it even important for us to know our purpose? When we start with why and begin with the end in mind, we are far more likely to have greater clarity and focus about how we want to live our lives, greater health and happiness, increased resilience and a life lived with integrity.

Leaders who know their purpose also tend to be clear on what success means to them. Success means different things to different people, and how we measure success is linked to our values and our stage of life. As discussed in Chapter Three, our values stay the same, but our priorities often change. Our measures of success can also vary, depending on current circumstances.

> When you know your purpose, you open yourself to possibility.

When you know your purpose, you open yourself to possibility.

My purpose (in case you're wondering) is to help people, particularly leaders and emerging leaders, become more connectable. Because when we connect, we are healthier and happier, have stronger relationships and are better humans.

## Manage your energy

Life is a marathon, not a sprint, and to give ourselves the best chance of a long and healthy life, we need to understand and manage our personal energy.

Time is finite. Energy is not. We can refuel and refresh our bodies, minds and souls, but we can't get back time.

Think about what gives you energy.

Some of the common elements include nutrition, exercise, sleep, doing work you love and being mentally fulfilled, and spending time with people who lift you up.

And now think about how you spend your day.

Are you all-systems-go from the moment you get up? Do you have a jam-packed to-do list? A never-ending collection of emails to answer? A calendar filled with meetings?

If this sounds familiar, it's no wonder you're tired.

In Chapter Three, we met Ben Vasiliou, CEO of Youth Projects, who shared how he brought his energy to work. Ben also told me how he manages his personal energy. 'I wear my heart on my sleeve, so you can see and feel my energy quite easily. This means I need to take care of myself to lead by example. I'm really serious about good food, good nutrition, good water and good sleep. Having enough exercise and socialising with the right people at the right time also helps manage my energy flow, and I keep a close check on all of those things.'

If you want to manage your energy better, think about the following:

- Look at the big picture: What are your big goals? Does everything need to be done today, or can you spread it over time?

- Make time every day to look after yourself: Prepare and eat nourishing foods, drink enough water, exercise, and get enough sleep. Think of your body as a car – if you don't put the right fuel in, it will conk out.
- Know what – and who – sustains and drains you: What effect do people have? I'm an introvert, which means my batteries recharge when I spend time alone. Work out what you need, and make sure you get it.
- Pace yourself: Structure your day, so you don't hit the 3pm slump. Productivity hacks can help with this, such as Pomodoro, where you work for twenty-five minutes and then take a five-minute break. Building regular breaks, including morning and afternoon tea and a decent lunch break, will help manage your energy.
- Step away from screens: Devices and the apps we use are designed to be addictive. Over time they will sap your energy. Be conscious of how much time you spend in front of a screen and whether it is really necessary.

## Work on your mindset

Tennis great Martina Navratilova was once asked how she maintained her focus, physique and sharp game, even at the age of forty-three. Her response? 'The ball doesn't know how old I am.'

Your mindset is your frame of mind, and it can propel you forward or hold you back. It's the assortment of thoughts and beliefs that shape your responses and interpretations. Your mindset affects how you think, what you feel, what you do, and what you say. Over time, these beliefs become your truth. As discussed in Chapter Three, they can become the stories you tell yourself.

Carol Dweck is a psychologist and the author of *Mindset*.[74] She believes people have either a fixed mindset or a growth mindset. When our mindset is fixed, we assume we cannot change in any meaningful way. We believe we are what we are, and that avoiding failure allows us to maintain our sense of intelligence. Conversely, with a growth mindset, we embrace and thrive on challenges. We seek to stretch our abilities and see failure as a springboard to future success.

Mindset develops from an early age. Were you encouraged to learn or criticised for 'failing'? Were you taught to look pretty or explore the world (and perhaps get a bit dirty)?

It's not too late if you feel your mindset is more fixed than growth. With effort, you can change it.

One way to do this is to replace negative words with the phrase 'not yet'. In her TED talk, *The Power of Believing You Can Improve*,[75] Dweck describes the power of yet in a high school where students had to pass a number of courses to graduate. If they didn't pass, they got the grade 'Not yet.' She said, 'And I thought that was fantastic, because if you get a failing grade, you think, I'm nothing, I'm nowhere. But if you get the grade 'Not yet', you understand that you're on a learning curve. It gives you a path into the future.'

There are other types of mindsets besides fixed and growth.

Fully connected leaders have what Cathy Burke, author of *Lead In*,[76] describes as a leader's mindset. This 'inspires others to act. You know what you stand for, and you become the standard that you uphold. You don't entertain behaviours, words or attitudes that undermine that.'

With a leader's mindset, we embrace and thrive on challenges. We seek to stretch our abilities and see failure as a springboard to future success. We want to live up to our potential.

Cathy Burke offers a four-step approach to developing a leader's mindset:

1. Notice the stories you tell yourself that stop you from achieving your goals.
2. Question your unhelpful beliefs and ask what you have made your situation mean – is it true?
3. Choose to break from unconscious reactions and choose how you want to show up. This is your chance to forge a different path.
4. Action is where you demonstrate that choice. Taking action strengthens new mindsets and provides an opportunity for feedback and reflection.

## Self-motivation checklist

- ☐ I am clear on what motivates me
- ☐ I know what I want to achieve
- ☐ I am prepared to take imperfect action and start
- ☐ I have mapped out a plan to achieve my goals
- ☐ I have chunked my plan into ninety-day actions
- ☐ I will be ruthless about distractions, including my phone and other devices
- ☐ I can track my progress
- ☐ I am ready to celebrate my wins.

A printable version of this checklist is available at www.melkettle.com/fullyconnected

# Reflection questions

What motivates you?
___
___
___

What stops you from taking action?
___
___
___

What habits and routines would help you to achieve better outcomes?
___
___
___

What internal triggers distract you?
___
___
___

List three ways to celebrate your wins.

How can you better manage your energy?

How is your mindset holding you back?

# Chapter Five

# Prioritise Self-care

As a child, I remember my father coming home from work and commenting that his day was full of meetings, so he didn't get any work done. It took a long time to understand what he meant, but I got it by the time I was in my late twenties and in my first management role. I mean, I *really* got it.

I was in the events world – managing a team of six, responsible for organising close to three hundred events each year. It was high pressure and stressful.

It was rare that I didn't work from 7am until well after 7pm. An average day had five hours of meetings, three hours dealing with staffing and people issues, and a couple of hours of actual work. All topped off with two hours in the car commuting between my home, my office and my client's office, some 11kms apart. It doesn't sound like much, but this was Sydney during the late 1990s. The Harbour Tunnel was being built, construction was rampant as the city prepared to host the 2000 Olympics, and traffic was *hell*. The shining light was being entertained by Wendy

Harmer on the radio for my morning commute, so at least I was laughing every day.

Life seemed glamorous on the outside, but it was hard. I had big responsibilities, big budgets to manage and big expectations to meet. My body and mind were slowly starting to unravel.

It's hardly surprising given I was working twelve-hour days, stressed out, living on a diet of alcohol, caffeine and far too many McDonald's and Thai takeaways. Too few vegetables, too little exercise and generally less than six hours of sleep each night.

I was also crying all the time, struggling to sleep, and had lots of weird dreams – often where I was driving a car at high speed with no brakes! I felt general queasiness and nausea most days, and I knew I wasn't pregnant. I had a nervous tick under one eye, and my hands shook.

Unbeknown to me, my blood pressure was escalating. However, it wasn't until I had significant chest pains, almost hourly, that I was frightened enough to head to the doctor. You know, after I'd been having them for a month or two – or maybe even three.

My very kind doctor lovingly, if somewhat brutally, said: 'You're completely burnt out and on the verge of a breakdown. If you don't make some major lifestyle changes, you will probably have a stroke before you turn thirty.' He also diagnosed me with mild depression, which was almost a bigger shock.

Three months before my thirtieth birthday, this was the wake-up call I needed.

And you know the worst part? I mostly hated my job, the pressure it placed on me, living in Sydney, with no time to have a life. I hated that I was eating rubbish food so often. I hated that I drank probably ten bottles of wine a week. Usually alone. I hated that I was single. I hated that I had forgotten what a hobby was and had no time to do what I loved. Actually, I had forgotten what I loved because I was so mired in unhappiness and loneliness.

On the plus side, I loved my team, and had a pretty good boss. We were a fantastic team, and we stuck by each other to get a phenomenal amount done, bolstering each other during the really shit times. That's why I stayed in the job as long as I did.

This employer valued us and rewarded us for arriving early, staying late and working twelve-hour days. On one of my last days, after eleven hours in the office, I left work at 6pm. My boss asked if I was leaving early because I was sick. Sadly, he wasn't even joking.

## Busy is the enemy of kind

We live in a world with the underlying belief that we must always be busy. It is seen as a badge of honour. A marker of self-worth. A sign of achievement.

> Practicing self-care is an antidote to busy.

Being busy is often confused with being productive. Busy means you have a lot on or are undertaking many activities. It doesn't mean you are being productive. Or focused. Or creative. Or kind to yourself.

I know it's time to take a break when I find myself doing 'busy' tasks when I should be working. Taking out the bins, tidying my office, menu planning for the week, trying to get my inbox to zero. Granted, most of these tasks need to be done (okay, maybe not inbox zero), but not when I'm up against a book deadline or should be focusing on preparing for the workshop I'm running tomorrow.

Being busy can be a sign of overwhelm or over-scheduling. And it can negatively affect your health, your relationships and your life.

Practicing self-care is an antidote to busy.

## Why care?

Self-care means giving yourself permission to pause, take a breath and focus on yourself, even briefly.

When we practice self-care, we do things that make us feel good. It's essential for our physical health, mental health and emotional wellbeing, and is clinically proven to reduce or eliminate anxiety and depression, and reduce stress at home and work.

It allows us to reconnect with ourselves, which makes us more effective as it gives us improved concentration, happiness and energy, and reduces negative emotions such as frustration and anger.

Demonstrating that we are important enough to practice self-care also sets an excellent example for our employees, colleagues, kids, and others who look up to us.

A large part of self-care is placing ourselves as our top priority – at least for some of the time. Prioritising ourselves helps us to reinvigorate ourselves, so we have more energy and focus for the other parts of our lives.

If you're looking for a role model, consider basketball player LeBron James. He is one of the NBA's five oldest players in the 2021-22 season, and he has reached this pinnacle by investing in himself. He allegedly spends US$1.5 million a year to look after himself physically and mentally. This investment means he is in the best condition to keep playing. Given he earns more than US$40 million a year playing for the LA Lakers, it seems like a worthwhile expense.[77]

While LeBron James has loads of money and can afford vast sums to invest in self-care, it doesn't actually *need* to be expensive. It's not all about champagne, massages and pedicures. Not that I would say no to any of those. Self-care is about creating the time and space to focus on yourself.

Self-care also looks different for everyone. What's soothing to me could be stressful to you. One of my most effective self-care methods is to have a walk on the beach and a quick swim in the ocean. It restores my energy and refreshes me enormously. Some of my friends love a pyjama day in front of Netflix. One of my clients loves bushwalking. Others go for long bike rides.

An important part of emotional self-care is practicing self-compassion. Dr Kristin Neff, a leading self-compassion researcher, suggests being kind to ourselves is one of three elements of self-compassion (the others are mindfulness and common humanity). Recognise your imperfections and that life can sometimes be a bit tough, and go gently on yourself.[78]

According to Dr Neff, 'having compassion for oneself is really no different than having compassion for others... Self-compassion involves acting the same way towards yourself when you are having a difficult time, fail, or notice something you don't like about yourself.'

We have compassion for others when we notice they are suffering. Most of us feel compassion when a friend tells us of a difficult situation. We feel moved by their plight, and we respond to their pain. We want to help them by demonstrating love, care and kindness. When our friends make mistakes, we offer understanding and forgiveness rather than cruelty and harsh judgement. We often feel grateful that we aren't struggling in the same way, however, we recognise that adversity, imperfection and anguish are part of life, and that they could easily happen to us too.

What endlessly fascinates me is that we are often our own worst enemies.

> We are often our own worst enemies.

Why, when we are suffering, do we continue to put ourselves down? Why do we listen to the mean little voice in our head that says, 'Of course that happened to you, you're just not good enough'? Or the voice that says 'you'll never get that promotion' or 'why on earth would you think that your idea is a good one' or 'you're such a loser' or 'really, again? Why didn't you know better?'

We would never say those words to our friends! So why do we say them to ourselves?

Kate Billing is the co-founder and creative director of Blacksmith,[79] a boutique leadership development practice based in Auckland, New Zealand. A few years ago, I did her excellent Tune-In workshop. One of the tools she uses to manage the nasty little voice in our heads is to humanise and name it. I named mine Gertrude, and she looks like an evil witch, with a long pointy face and an ugly hooked nose.

Today, when Gertrude starts to sneak into my head, I tell her to f*ck right off, and she goes back into the very tiny box in a corner of my brain where I don't notice her.

How do we turn off this negative self-talk and turn it into a positive? How do we talk to ourselves like someone we love?

I'm not saying it's easy because it's not, especially if you're used to talking to yourself like one of those mean girls from high school. What can we do to be kinder to ourselves? To love ourselves more? To remove the blame and shame?

## Goodbye guilt!

We can start by getting rid of feeling guilty.

And we can definitely lose the expression 'a guilty pleasure'. It's designed to make us feel bad when we do things we enjoy, whether eating that third chocolate biscuit or binge-watching another series on Netflix.

We need time to do what we love without any overriding feeling of guilt.

Guilt is attached to judgement. As one who was raised a Catholic, I have spent many, many years feeling guilty and judged by others for not doing what's expected of me. It's easy to feel guilty for eating the 'wrong' foods, taking a 'me' day off work, and spending money on something we want rather than something we need.

When we attach our guilt to someone else's judgement, we tell ourselves that their opinion of us is more worthy than our view of ourselves. We are far better off when we own our decisions, don't beat ourselves up over our actions, and practice some self-compassion.

A great way to get rid of guilt is to focus on positivity and things that give joy and fulfilment.

## From FOMO to JOMO

I joined Twitter in April 2009 and a few months later saw a barrage of tweets about the #BlogHerFood Conference in the US. As a newly minted food blogger, I had *major* FOMO (fear of missing out). So much so that I was determined to attend the 2010 conference. This was not the first time FOMO would lead me to decide on a course of action. Fortunately, my #BlogHerFood experience was extremely positive. I learned a lot and created some great friendships.

Sadly, the same cannot be said for many other decisions I've made because I didn't want to miss out.

FOMO is real and can be dangerous. You know you are deep in the weeds with it when you want to do everything and be everywhere while achieving very little.

Researcher Volkan Dogan[80] has found that FOMO is linked to how individuals understand and experience the world, and what they feel they are being excluded from. He identified a clear connection between self-perception on social media and FOMO.

Many people on social media show false and often inauthentic versions of themselves, so it is not surprising that FOMO can lead to feelings of inadequacy and imposter syndrome, increased stress, social anxieties, and an unnecessary busyness in our lives.

Fortunately, there is an antidote. JOMO – the joy of missing out – is becoming increasingly desirable.

JOMO occurs when we consciously decide to make time for other things equal to or better than what we are missing out on. The first step in embracing JOMO is acknowledging that you might need to change how you live your life.

Embracing JOMO requires regular practice. You need to unlearn the need to be constantly doing things. It will probably require a recalibration of your view of success and setting some new boundaries.

Moving from FOMO to JOMO is not always easy, but it's worth it.

## Self-care leads to resilience

The American Psychological Association defines resilience as 'the process of adapting well in the face of adversity, trauma, tragedy, threats or significant sources of stress – such as family and relationship problems, serious health problems or workplace and financial stressors. It means bouncing back from difficult experiences.'[81]

Caring for ourselves gives us tools and resources to manage stress. Just as we do when dealing with a physical injury or illness.

In my twenties, my stress-coping mechanisms all involved alcohol. I've been trying to think how else I used to manage my stress, and nope, alcohol was it. I'm not proud to say that I could drink a bottle of wine and feel completely sober. Do you know how I realised I had better coping mechanisms in place? A few years later, I slurred my words after a single glass of wine – and it wasn't an overly large glass.

The more we practice *positive* self-care and build it into our regular routines, the better we are equipped to handle stress and trauma when it comes our way.

# The foundations of self-care

Self-care can mean many things to different people, but I reckon there are five core foundations that we need to get right, if we are to be alright.

## Foundation #1: Be aware of your health

Physical health is often the easiest to look after. It's usually quite obvious when things start to go wrong. We feel unwell, unexpectedly lose or gain weight, or experience physical pain.

Mental health issues can be a bit trickier to identify. Good mental health means being able to experience the good and bad aspects of life and cope with them in a psychologically and emotionally healthy way.

## Make regular medical checks non-negotiable.

Our physical and mental health are linked. A deficit in one can lead to negative consequences in the other. If we don't get enough of the right foods, exercise or sleep, our mental health can decline. Even consuming too much sugar, cigarettes, alcohol, and other drugs can negatively impact mental health.

I'm sure I'm not the only one who has learned the hard way what can happen when you let the basics of food, sleep and exercise slip. It's not pretty.

If it's been a while since you last had a regular health check, perhaps it's time to book one in.

Make regular medical checks non-negotiable. Yes, it's time-consuming. Yes, it can be uncomfortable, awkward and embarrassing. And yes, it can be expensive. But I promise that the costs of cancer, cardiovascular disease, diabetes, and more, are far greater. The costs aren't only related to medical appointments; they're also about missed work, lost opportunities and the negative impacts on your quality of life.

If you notice any body bits have changed, get them checked out. In 2013 I was diagnosed with a level two melanoma after noticing a dodgy spot on my leg. I immediately had it checked and biopsied by my doctor. The surgeon later told me it was very aggressive, and if I hadn't had a biopsy as soon as I'd noticed it, I probably would have died within a year (yes, that *is* as confronting as it sounds). For those who think, 'My skin is dark, and I tan easily,' then let me remind you that Bob Marley died from melanoma when he was only thirty-six.

One of my friends takes a week off work every July for self-care. During this week, she has all the annual medical tests she needs – a general check-up with her doctor and appointments with her gynaecologist, dermatologist, dentist and optometrist. She also books a massage, some beautician appointments, a couple of lunch dates with friends, and goes to the movies or the theatre. She balances fun with the necessary and has done so for more than twenty years.

The point is this: as we age, we should all have annual health checks to stay on top of things. We take our cars for a service at least once a year, so make do the same for your body. It can be a lot messier and more expensive to fix when things go wrong!

Your doctor can advise you on what health checks you should be having and how frequently.

### Don't forget to manage your stress

An essential part of looking after your health is understanding and managing your stress levels.

Increasingly, my clients tell me about rising stress levels they feel personally and notice within their teams. This leads to overwhelm, anxiety and, in some cases, depression and burnout.

A colleague recently suggested that your manager has a greater impact on your health than your doctor. Is it any wonder that leaders need to understand what causes and triggers stress? We need to recognise the signs, so we can take steps to reduce it – for ourselves and our people.

While some stress is essential to prevent boredom and encourage productivity, too much can be dangerous.

Chronic stress occurs when the level exceeds what we can comfortably sustain. For example, increased and continuous pressure at work can lead to chronic stress, as can uncertainty caused by a global pandemic.

Stress provides us with plenty of warning signs. It's like the metaphor of the feather, the brick and the truck.

My *feather* was that I was consistently lying awake at night, worried about all the work I needed to do. The *brick* was having constant chest pains and my doctor giving me a warning. I'm fortunate that I didn't get hit by the *truck*, unlike one friend who had a stress-related stroke in her late twenties, or another friend who had a SCAD (spontaneous coronary artery dissection) heart attack at fifty-three. (I had never heard of a SCAD heart attack until this friend had one two years ago. The trigger is usually a short period of extreme stress. More than ninety per cent of people afflicted are female, in their forties or early fifties, appear healthy and have no other risk factors.)

With good levels of self-awareness, we are more likely to recognise the feathers. Some of the more common are:

- Consistently working long hours. An occasional ten to twelve-hour day is fine, but continually working more than eight hours a day means something is wrong. This level of work is just not sustainable.
- A decline in work performance. You start doing 'busy' work rather than deep work.
- You're moody and grumpy with increased mood swings, and you might cry a lot.
- Difficulty sleeping – either getting to sleep or staying asleep. (My rule is that if I have three consecutive sleepless nights due to worrying about work, it's time to get another job or get rid of that client.)
- Headaches
- Excessive hair loss
- Drinking more alcohol or coffee than usual
- Chest pains or heart palpitations
- Grinding your teeth (My dentist told me she fitted more patients for mouth guards during the first eighteen months of Covid than in the previous fifteen years.)
- A feeling of overwhelming sadness
- The inability to make even simple decisions.

If you notice any of these symptoms for a prolonged period, get to your doctor. And if you are struggling with anxiety and not sure what to do next, please seek professional support.

In Australia, you can contact Lifeline on 13 11 14 or use its anonymous online chat service (available between 7pm and midnight AEST) at www.lifeline.org.au. You can also visit Beyond Blue's website, www.beyondblue.org.au, for additional support. For crisis assistance, call 000.

Talking with someone (such as your GP or physician) who tells you you're not going completely crazy can be therapeutic and reassuring. Your doctor can refer you to a psychologist or psychiatrist and prescribe medications. In Australia, you may be eligible for a Mental Health Treatment Plan, which gives you Medicare rebates for support from psychologists and other health professionals. For more information, go to www.healthdirect.gov.au.

A few years ago, I was going through an extremely stressful personal situation. Making a phone call to book an appointment with a psychologist immediately helped me feel more in control. And the support she gave me in that first consultation lifted the heavy weight that was crushing me.

### Reducing overwhelm

Many practical strategies can reduce feelings of overwhelm, especially if you feel your stress is building, but you don't yet need professional support. These have worked for me over the years. Try them and add your own:

- Get some exercise. A walk on the beach does wonders as the fresh air gets endorphins moving. A daggy dance in the living room to loud seventies music has a similar effect.
- Spend time every day doing something just for you. Even fifteen minutes can make a difference.
- Laugh. Anxiety disappears, at least temporarily, when you watch a comedy. Check out the TV series *Ted Lasso* if you haven't seen it yet.
- Get chickens (or another pet). Okay, this isn't going to be possible for everyone, but the antics of our chickens made me laugh every day. It's just a shame they ran away when I tried to pick them up for a cuddle. There's plenty of research about the therapeutic benefits of having a pet, so it's worth considering. If it's not possible to have one where you live, ask friends with pets if you can spend time with them. As we are now, sadly, a chicken-less household (thanks to no backyard), I talk to my neighbour's chickens. You could also visit a cat café or become a dog walker for the RSPCA, as one of my friends has done.
- Go outside and have some time in nature as this will boost your immune system and reduce blood pressure and stress. Shinrin-yoku (forest bathing) is a trend that started in Japan in the 1980s in response to Japan's public health crisis from overwork

resulting in death. It was a way to support people who were burning out from the tech boom.
- If you can't get outside, bring the green in. Studies have shown that even seeing green plants can have a restorative benefit. Perhaps unsurprisingly, Covid lockdowns turned buying indoor plants into a pandemic trend.[82]
- Step away. Literally, step away and remove yourself from the stressful situation. Go for a quick walk or work from another location for an hour or two.
- Breathe. Try meditation, yoga or breathwork to help regulate your breathing.

## Foundation #2: Get the basics right

For me, the basics are having the right nutrition, getting some exercise, and getting enough sleep. If one of these is temporarily out of alignment, the other two can help pick up the pieces. But if two or more are consistently dysfunctional, you're asking for trouble.

Let's look briefly at each of these.

### Food and nutrition

I'm not a dietician, so I won't tell you what to eat, especially as we all respond differently to foods. If you're unsure, work out how your body reacts to various foods, and if necessary, seek the advice of a registered dietician.

Knowing what to eat and when is more confusing now than ever. I read an article years ago that said Americans find doing their taxes easier than knowing what they should and shouldn't eat. That's not surprising, given we are bombarded with marketing messages by big food companies. Kellogg's, McDonald's and Coca-Cola have significantly more money to spend on educating us than our fruit and vegetable growers and suppliers.

If you buy packaged food, pre-prepared or other time-saving meals, learn to read the nutritional label on the packet. If you eat out a lot, don't be afraid to ask what's in the meal you're ordering. One of the reasons restaurant and café food usually tastes so great is because chefs add liberal amounts of butter, salt and sugar to improve the flavour. I'll never forget watching the *MasterChef Australia* episode when George Calombaris demonstrated making mashed potatoes. For every 250g of potato, he used 250g of butter! (Regular makers of mashed potatoes will know this is *a lot* of butter.)

We also need to consider what we drink and whether we are drinking enough water. Insufficient water can leave us with brain fog, a lack of energy and digestive issues. Drinking the right amount of water can also help with weight loss if that's something you're trying to do.

Be aware that too much caffeine, alcohol, and sugary drinks can also negatively affect your physical and mental health.

## Make time for exercise and movement

Movement is about more than exercise. It's about taking regular breaks from our computer – or the couch – to move our bodies. This is important because our joints and ligaments stiffen as we age, and we lose muscle mass. I know I feel physical pain if I spend more than an hour sitting at my desk without standing up for a quick stretch!

For healthy adults, it's suggested we are physically active on most, if not all, days of the week.

Research shows we move ninety per cent less than our ancestors did a hundred years ago. According to endocrinologist Dr James Levine, obese people sit on average two-and-a-half hours more every day than thinner people.[83] And when you sit for long periods, your body goes into storage mode, which can even make your bottom bigger.

From a mental health perspective, Dr Levine says that people who sit more are also more prone to depression, and if you have a mental illness, it can become worse. This is not great news for those of us who are desk-bound, love a good Netflix binge or spend too many hours sitting while commuting to work... #notnamingnames

Some of my favourite ways of moving more are:

- having my printer in a different room to my computer

- walking around the house when I'm on the phone (ten minutes is about 1,000 steps)
- only listening to my favourite podcasts when I'm walking
- catching up with friends for a walk and a takeaway coffee rather than sitting in a café.

### *Prioritising sleep and rest*

I am super passionate about sleep and rest. I reckon I could give multiple TED talks on the negative impacts of not getting enough sleep and not taking regular breaks. I need my eight hours at least four or five times a week to feel human. Menopause is not kind to sleep patterns, and it's no surprise that I recently heard sleep described as a performance-enhancing drug.

A lack of sleep debilitates our mental and physical health, including heart disease, obesity and depression. Not getting enough sleep is like being in a permanent state of jetlag, and those of us who remember the joys of international travel know how awful that feels.

> **Poor sleep behaviour is often an individual choice.**

Poor sleep behaviour is often an individual choice.

The Sleep Health Foundation[84] estimates that four out of ten Australians don't get enough sleep (on average, we get 6.5 hours a night, with some twelve per cent having 5.5 hours or less), and twenty per cent suffer excessive daytime sleepiness. A study published in the medical journal *Sleep* found that six hours or less of slumber could be as bad as not sleeping at all.[85]

What causes our lack of sleep? I mentioned in Chapter One that the biggest competitor of Netflix is sleep, so I am sure you won't be surprised that streaming services are partly to blame.

There are also times when it's hard to get enough sleep – when you're a new parent, feeling the effects of jetlag or going through peri or post menopause and your sleep is disrupted thanks to the joys of raging hormones and night sweats (#sarcasmalert). Sharing a bed with someone else can also lead to a lack of sleep – there's a reason one of my friends has a separate bedroom from her partner. (When I got up this morning, my husband said, 'You're lucky I love you so much'. Apparently, I lay on my back snoring while he tried to get back to sleep at 5am. I told him it was only fair since most nights I lie awake listening to him snoring.)

There is plenty of wearable tech available to track sleep. I've recently bought an Oura ring (you can only buy them online from www.oura.com), and the insights it gives me about the quality and quantity of sleep I'm getting are illuminating.

## FULLY CONNECTED

If you're tired all the time but believe you're getting enough sleep, then see your doctor. You could have a serious sleep disorder, such as sleep apnoea.

Getting enough rest isn't only about enough sleep. We need to make sure we give our brains time to rest during the day, too. Too many of us operate at full steam during the day without heeding our body's need for rest. And I don't mean a quick nap – although I'm certainly not averse to that.

Our brains thrive when they have time to rest. As mentioned in Chapter Two, we make more than 30,000 decisions a day, so the cognitive load is immense. If we don't take time to rest our brain during the day, our performance, mood, and physical and mental health suffer.

> **Rest is about more than sleep.**

As Ferris Jabr wrote in *Scientific American*,[86] 'Downtime replenishes the brain's stores of attention and motivation, encourages productivity and creativity, and is essential to both achieve our highest levels of performance and simply form stable memories in everyday life... moments of respite may even be necessary to keep one's moral compass in working order and maintain a sense of self.'

One technique I use to give my brain a break is the 52:17 method. That means I work hard on a task (or a group of tasks) for 52 minutes, then have a screen-free break for

17 minutes. During that time, I might go for a quick walk, make a phone call, go to the bathroom, make a cup of tea, or chat with a colleague. I find that my brain is still productive at 4pm on the days I employ this technique. On the days I don't, I flag after lunch.

Many other time-based productivity tools are available, too. Experiment and find one that works for you.

And let's not forget how important it is to take regular holidays. When we regularly take time off work, our productivity improves, our stress reduces, and we enjoy life more.

We typically get four weeks (or twenty workdays) of paid annual leave in Australia. However, most of us don't take all our leave each year. Plan to use your holidays and put them in your diary. I've found that unless I pencil in holidays at the start of the year, chances are, I won't have any.

I love Richard Branson's philosophy on taking a vacation: 'Maintaining focus on having fun isn't just about rest and recuperation: When you go on vacation, your routine is interrupted; the places you go and the new people you meet can inspire you in unexpected ways.'[87]

## Foundation #3: Have clear boundaries and stick to them

I used to be a yes girl. I'd say yes to everything.

Volunteer on a committee? Check.

Coffee meetings to pick my brain? Check.

Travel to your side of town for a meeting even though it inconvenienced me? Check.

> Saying no creates boundaries.

Take every work opportunity, whether paid or unpaid? Check.

A date with a guy I didn't really like? Check. (Maybe he had cute friends.)

I was a people pleaser who didn't know how to say no, and on the rare occasion I did, I felt I was letting people down.

We risk teetering on the edge of burnout when we say yes to everything. When we start to say no, we take back some control over our lives.

Saying no creates boundaries around what we will and won't do. Boundaries are essential to healthy relationships and a healthy life. They can help you make decisions based on what is best for you. This is a vital part of self-care. Not having healthy boundaries can impact all areas of your life, including your physical and emotional health, your finances, and your relationships.

Imagine your boundaries as a fence around what you want to protect. Sometimes you need to open the gate to slip out, but mostly you want that gate closed to protect what is most important to you.

Our boundaries can be personal or professional, physical or emotional.

Here are some examples of healthy boundaries.

- Prioritising time every day for self-care. My friend Christina has a non-negotiable morning routine that includes looking after her body, mind and soul. Nothing prevents this from happening.
- Limiting (or eliminating) the amount of time you spend with negative people or people who suck your energy. If these people must be in your life, how can you set boundaries to have some control over how much or how often you need to interact with them?
- Restricting the amount of time you spend on social media and/or in front of screens when not at work. Develop a personal tech policy with guidelines. These might include device-free zones and times, and switching your phone to flight mode to focus on deep work and your loved ones. Try reading paperbacks instead of e-books. Set a limit on your hours of Netflix each week. How about no work email on weekends? My family and friends know that most nights my phone is on silent after 8pm and doesn't get switched on again until at least 8am. I also frequently leave my phone on silent during the day so I can focus on deep work without distractions.

- Deciding when you work and when you don't – especially after the workday has officially ended. Will you work weekends and public holidays? Are you expected to answer emails and the work phone after hours? Do you expect this from your team?
- Saying no more often to things you don't really want to do.

As the Brazilian author, Paulo Coelho writes, 'When you say 'yes' to others, make sure you are not saying 'no' to yourself.'

While no *is* a complete sentence, it can be helpful to learn to say it with more elegance. Say it firmly and politely, and you won't have the recipient continually begging you to say yes!

These are a few ways that work for me:

- No, thank you. (In a firm and polite voice that the asker won't argue with – and then if they say 'are you sure?' you can say yes).
- I am not available. I am already committed on that date.
- This is not the right project/opportunity for me.
- I am at capacity.

My friend Kate is great at saying no. She channels writer Derek Sivers, believing if it isn't a *hell yes*, then it's a *hell no!*[88]

## Foundation #4: Do something every day that brings you joy

Seeking joy should be a guiding principle for us all. Knowing what brings you joy and doing some of these activities every day will recharge your personal batteries and increase your energy.

Research tells us that when we focus on joy, even for as little as thirty seconds a day, our stress hormones reduce, oxygen flow to our bodies increases, and we are happier. Joy and happiness also lead to a longer lifespan.

When we do things that we love and that provide a sense of achievement, we automatically feel happier. But perhaps more importantly, when we love and are kind to ourselves, we are more likely to be kind and loving towards others.

You have control over your happiness. Waking each day, you can choose to be happy or grumpy. Given our bias toward negativity, can you intentionally choose happy?

> **You have control over your happiness.**

Like many, Sarah was horribly challenged by the Covid lockdowns and the monotony of working from her small apartment, kid-wrangling her two little girls, and dealing with a loved one's health concerns. When I asked what she was doing to get through, Sarah said every night before going to bed, she planned to do something she loved the next day. It might have been a phone call with a friend, reading a new novel, or ordering takeout from her favourite restaurant. Doing this meant she went to sleep with something to look forward to.

This small kindness to herself each day gave her the joy she needed to keep going.

There are many ways to add joy to your day; here are a few:

- do something you love
- disconnect from social media (temporarily, at least)
- spend time in nature
- read a good book
- listen to music
- spend time with people you love
- exercise
- sleep
- volunteer
- watch the sun rise or set
- phone a friend
- meditate
- laugh.

Make a list of all the things that bring you joy. Do what Sarah does. Before you go to bed, choose one to do tomorrow, so you fall asleep smiling, knowing you have something to look forward to.

## Foundation #5: Practice gratitude

When life is going well, gratitude allows us to celebrate and amplify our positivity and our success. When life is difficult, gratitude can help us through challenging times.

> We gain resilience when we practice gratitude.

Did you know that practicing gratitude for as little as thirty seconds each day can reduce your stress hormones, increase oxygen flow to your body and make you happier? It can also increase your energy, improve your mood, make you feel more optimistic and boost your self-esteem.

We gain resilience when we practice gratitude.

Simple ways to practice gratitude include:

- Keep a gratitude journal. At the end of the day, write down at least three things you are grateful for.
- When you get up in the morning, spend the first five minutes sitting somewhere quiet and reflecting on the sights and sounds around you. What can you hear? What can you smell? What can you see?
- Be grateful for the simple things – people who love you, access to food, clean water, and shelter. Did you know that 2.4 billion people worldwide don't have access to a toilet? Every day I'm grateful that

I do. And that it's clean. And that I have a tap with running water to wash my hands afterwards.
- Appreciate who you are and what you do. The kindnesses you show people, the times you smile at strangers and when you graciously accept a compliment.

## Start with one thing

You might have reached the end of this section and thought, *'that's a lot'*. I'm not going to apologise, because you're right. It is. The good news is that you don't need to jump in and do it all at once. Start small and start with one thing.

The checklist at the end of this chapter outlines a list of things you could do. Go through the list and prioritise them based on what feels right for you. And then pick one to start with. If you're not sure where to start, my top tip would be to make a doctor's appointment for a health check and create a baseline to measure your future health.

Your second step might be to create a simple self-care kit to help you through the more challenging times. Four things are always in my kit. Herbal teas, chocolate, my sneakers (these are also the first things packed when I travel), and gin.

Think about what you might need in relation to each of your senses.

- Sight: Photos of people you love, a beautiful piece of art, a colouring book or a jigsaw.
- Sound: Music you love, a recording of your children telling you that they love you, a Spotify playlist that immediately cheers you up.
- Touch: A weighted or soft blanket, a book, a talisman, having a bath (immersing yourself in water).
- Taste: Chocolate, cheese, chips and gin are my go-to purchases when stress comes calling. What are yours?
- Smell: Essential oils, perfume, flowers.

You might want to make up an actual kit or just keep these things in the back of your mind for emergencies. Try a smaller version in your handbag, briefcase, travel bag, or desk.

As a child, I loved visiting my dad at work, not least because part of his self-care kit was a couple of blocks of good chocolate and a packet or two of chocolate biscuits. In my thirties, I visited his new office for the first time and went straight for his chocolate stash. He asked how I knew where it was, to which I replied, 'Dad, that's where it has been since I was seven. It's always been in the second drawer next to your chair'. Ten years later, my brother and I packed up Dad's office after he died. Jules was extremely impressed that I found the chocolate within seconds – especially as all that was left of the biscuits were crumbs.

You may need more than one self-care kit. Think about what you can keep in your office, at home, in the car, or in your handbag. That way, when you unexpectedly find yourself in a stressful situation, there is something to draw on to quickly calm yourself.

# The foundations of a self-care checklist

This list can be somewhat daunting, so prioritise and start with what's most important to you

- ☐ Book a doctor's appointment for a health check
- ☐ Plan a holiday, or at least block out dates in your calendar
- ☐ Be aware of what you're eating and drinking each day
- ☐ Make time for exercise
- ☐ Take regular breaks from your computer
- ☐ Create a morning routine
- ☐ Create a pre-bed routine
- ☐ Work out how much time you spend each day on your phone
- ☐ Delete one app from your phone
- ☐ Make a list of things you love to do and plan to do one of them today
- ☐ Start a gratitude journal.

A printable version of this checklist is available at www.melkettle.com/fullyconnected

## Reflection questions

What does your self-care routine currently look like?

_____

_____

_____

How could you improve your self-care routine?

_____

_____

_____

When did you last see your doctor, dentist or other healthcare practitioners? Do you know which health checks you should be having and how frequently?

_____

_____

_____

Are there feathers, bricks or trucks showing up in your life?

_____

_____

When did you last do something that filled you with joy?

What could fill you with joy today?

# Final words

I wrote this book because life as a leader can be hard. It's easy to get stuck on the treadmill and forget to slow down to step off and take a break.

We get busy and forget to take care of ourselves. Or worse, we start to lose our essence as we get caught up in our day-to-day world.

If you only take away one thing from this book, it should be to start prioritising yourself and doing things that bring you joy. Okay, so that's two things. But they go together.

My personal experience has taught me that it's not always that easy – especially if you have been taught to serve others before yourself.

If you get stuck, go back and re-read Chapter Two. Remember why you want to be a fully connected leader and the benefits it will bring to you and your team. I haven't mentioned family much throughout the book, but trust me, they will also benefit from the changes.

Change can be scary, especially when it requires deep work to get to know yourself better. But life is just too damn short to stay in survival mode.

I hope this book has helped you realise you have choices about how you live. And that you *are* worth the effort.

We need fully connected leaders more than ever – you deserve it, your workforce deserves it, and your customers deserve it. And, of course, your family deserves it.

Reading this book is your first step.

I look forward to seeing you take the next ones.

# References and Reading

This list includes some of my favourite books, blogs and podcasts. I've also included a few of my favourite menopause resources, just in case you're also going through that time of life.

I hope you enjoy them.

### Non-fiction books

Julia Banks, *PowerPlay*

Brené Brown, *Dare to Lead* (and all her books...)

Ruth Coker Burks, *All the Young Men*

Gabrielle Dolan, *Real Communication*

Glennon Doyle, *Untamed*

Nir Eyal, *Indistractable*

Elizabeth Gilbert, *Big Magic*

Julia Gillard and Ngozi Okonjo-Iweala, *Women and Leadership*

Florence Given, *Women Don't Owe You Pretty*

Vivek H. Murthy, *Together*

Rebecca Sparrow, *Find Your Tribe* (and all of Bec's books, especially her books for tween and teenage girls)

Abby Wambach, *Wolfpack*

## Podcasts

This Connected Life with me!

Chat10 Looks 3

Steph's Business Bookshelf

First Time Facilitator with Leanne Hughes

This Working Life with Lisa Leong

Unlocking Us and Dare to Lead with Brené Brown

FORTY with Those Two Girls

## Cookbooks

In case you feel the need to do some procrasti-cooking or procrasti-baking, these are my current favourite (and most used) cookbooks:

Hetty McKinnon, *Community* and *Neighbourhood* – truly spectacular vegetarian salads

Thomasina Miers, *Mexican Food Made Simple*

Jamie Oliver, *Jamie's America*

Yotam Ottolenghi – all his books are fantastic, however, my favourites are *Jerusalem* and *Plenty More*

### Fiction authors I love

Allison Brennan
Alafair Burke
Lisa Gardner
Laura Griffin
Clare Mackintosh
Jill Mansell
Kate Quinn
Karen Rose
Joanne Tracey

### Menopause resources

*The Menopause Manifesto,* Dr Jen Gunter
*This Changes Everything,* Niki Bezzant
*Don't Sweat It,* Nicky Pellegrino
*Hormone Repair Manual,* Lara Briden
*Just as Juicy* (www.justasjuicy.com), Mel Kettle
Australasian Menopause Society (www.menopause.org.au)

# Want more?

Thank you for reading *Fully Connected*.

If you have enjoyed the book and think I could support you and your organisation to become Fully Connected, I would love the opportunity to add value.

I can help with:

### Leadership training

My Connected Leadership Programs are designed to empower leaders and teams to connect with themselves and communicate with conviction, so they can engage and inspire their people. They range from short and one-off training sessions to lift your people, to a twelve-month program to transform and sustain.

### Strategic communication

I have worked with organisations to develop impactful communication strategies for more than twenty-five years. Today I work with executive teams, communication teams, boards and business owners to design and develop strategies that provide clarity and focus, to best enable them to achieve their goals.

## Speaker

Practical, pragmatic and real, I deliver presentations that cut through the clutter to focus on how we can fully connect with ourselves and with others. Topics include leadership, connection and communication.

## Coaching and mentoring

My Executive Coaching and Mentoring program is designed to specifically help female leaders aged 40-55 (ish) with the challenges they face. We work together so you can gain new perspectives, enabling more purposeful and consistent leadership communication, gain increased visibility and influence, and have an immediate, meaningful impact in your workplace.

## Please get in touch

> www.melkettle.com: subscribe to my newsletter and listen to my podcast
> www.melkettle.com/fullyconnected: download the workbook that accompanies this book.
> Email: hello@melkettle.com
> Phone: +61 404 600 889

## Connect with me on social media

> Twitter: @melkettle
> Instagram: @melkettle
> LinkedIn: melkettle

# Endnotes

1. Kettle, M. (2019-2022). *This Connected Life* [Podcast]. https://www.melkettle.com/podcast
2. Slaughter, A. (2012, July/August). Why Women Still Can't Have It All. *The Atlantic*. https://www.theatlantic.com/magazine/archive/2012/07/why-women-still-cant-have-it-all/309020
3. Walters, B. (2011, December 23). *20/20* [Television]. ABC.
4. Australian Psychological Society and Swinburne University. (2018). *Australian Loneliness Report, Psychology Week*, Australian Psychological Society and Swinburne University.
5. Cigna Newsroom. (2020). Cigna Takes Action To Combat The Rise Of Loneliness And Improve Mental Wellness In America. *Cigna*. https://www.cigna.com/newsroom/news-releases/2020/cigna-takes-action-to-combat-the-rise-of-loneliness-and-improve-mental-wellness-in-america
6. Saporito, T. J. (2012). It's Time to Acknowledge CEO Loneliness. *Harvard Business Review*. https://hbr.org/2012/02/its-time-to-acknowledge-ceo-lo
7. Medibank Research Series. (2011). *Sick at Work: The cost of presenteeism to your business and the economy*. Medibank. https://www.medibank.com.au/content/dam/client/documents/pdfs/sick_at_work.pdf
8. Regional TAM, OzTAM, Nielsen. (2016). *Australian Multi-Screen Report*. Regional TAM, OzTAM, Nielsen. https://oztam.com.au/documents/Other/Australian%20Multi%20Screen%20Report%20Q3%202016%20FINAL.pdf
9. Wheelwright, T. (2020, February 11). Cell Phone Behavior Survey: Are People Addicted to Their Phones? *Reviews.org*. https://www.reviews.org/mobile/cell-phone-addiction/

10. IDC Research Report. (2013). Always Connected: How Smartphones And Social Keep Us Engaged. *IDC*. https://www.nu.nl/files/IDC-Facebook%20Always%20Connected%20(1).pdf

11. Duke, É. and Montag, C. (2017). Smartphone addiction, daily interruptions and self-reported productivity. *Addictive Behaviors Reports, 6,* 90-95. https://doi.org/10.1016/j.abrep.2017.07.002

12. University of Derby. (2015, March 3). *Smartphones are addictive – reveals first UK study from the University of Derby*. www.derby.ac.uk. https://www.derby.ac.uk/news/2015/smartphones-are-addictive--reveals-first-uk-study-from-the-university-of-derby/

13. Kafka, P. (2017, April 17). Amazon? HBO? Netflix thinks its real competitor is... sleep. *Vox*. https://www.vox.com/2017/4/17/15334122/netflix-sleep-competitor-amazon-hbo

14. Smith, C. (2022, March 10). 90 Incredible Email Statistics. *DMR*. https://expandedramblings.com/index.php/email-statistics/

15. Walsh, L. (2020, July 19). The company banning Zoom meetings. *Australian Financial Review*. https://www.afr.com/companies/financial-services/the-company-banning-zoom-meetings-20200717-p55d27

16. Brown, B. (2020, March 20). Brené on FFTs (No. 1) [Podcast]. *Unlocking Us*. Cadence 13. https://brenebrown.com/podcast/brene-on-ffts/

17. Grant, A. (2021, April 19). There's a Name for the Blah You're Feeling: It's Called Languishing. *The New York Times*. https://www.nytimes.com/2021/04/19/well/mind/covid-mental-health-languishing.html

18. Krapivin, P. (2018, September 17). How Google's Strategy For Happy Employees Boosts Its Bottom Line. *Forbes*. https://www.forbes.com/sites/pavelkrapivin/2018/09/17/how-googles-strategy-for-happy-employees-boosts-its-bottom-line/?sh=7e4566f022fc

19. Merrill, R. M., Aldana, S. G., Pope, J. E., Anderson, D. R., Coberley, C. R., & Whitmer, and the HERO Research Stud, R. W. (2012). Presenteeism According to Healthy Behaviors, Physical

Health, and Work Environment. *Population Health Management*, 15(5), 293–301. https://doi.org/10.1089/pop.2012.0003

20. Dolan, G. (2019). *Real Communication: How to be you and lead true*. Wiley.
21. Buote, V. (2016, May 11). Most Employees Feel Authentic at Work, But It Can Take a While. *Harvard Business Review*. https://hbr.org/2016/05/most-employees-feel-authentic-at-work-but-it-can-take-a-while
22. Brown, B. (2019, June 1). *Brené Brown — The Call to Courage* [Video]. Netflix.
23. Fishkin, R. (2014, September 19). A Long, Ugly Year of Depression That's Finally Fading. *SparkToro*. https://sparktoro.com/blog/long-ugly-year-depression-thats-finally-fading/
24. Cournoyer, P. (2021, May 21). Be More Podcast: Vulnerability in the Workplace with Rand Fishkin. [Podcast]. *Workday*. https://blog.workday.com/en-us/2021/be-more-podcast-vulnerability-in-the-workplace-with-rand-fishkin.html
25. US Army. (2015). *FM 6-22: Leader Development*. Headquarters, Department of the Army. https://www.milsci.ucsb.edu/sites/secure.lsit.ucsb.edu.mili.d7/files/sitefiles/fm6_22.pdf
26. Gentry, W.A., Weber, T.J., Sadri, G. (2016). *Empathy in the Workplace: A Tool for Effective Leadership*. Center for Creative Leadership.
27. Baker, W. (2016, September 15). The More You Energize Your Coworkers, the Better Everyone Performs. *Harvard Business Review*. https://hbr.org/2016/09/the-energy-you-give-off-at-work-matters
28. Bradberry, T. (2016, June 28). Why The Best Leaders Have Conviction. *Forbes*. https://www.forbes.com/sites/travisbradberry/2016/06/28/why-the-best-leaders-have-conviction/?sh=44c41891c8da

29. Cassidy, F. (2017, December 15). Counting the cost of inefficient communication. *Raconteur*. https://www.raconteur.net/sponsored/counting-the-cost-of-inefficient-communication/
30. Towers Watson. (2010). Capitalizing on Effective Communication How Courage, Innovation and Discipline Drive Business Results in Challenging Times. Communication ROI Study Report. *Towers Watson*. http://benefitcommunications.com/upload/downloads/Capitalizing_on_Effective_Communication_-_Towers_Watson_survey.pdf
31. Kennedy, J. T., & Jain-Link, P. (2021, June 21). What Does It Take to Build a Culture of Belonging? *Harvard Business Review*. https://hbr.org/2021/06/what-does-it-take-to-build-a-culture-of-belonging
32. de Morree, P., & Minnaar, J. (2017). *How to build a workplace people love*. Family Business Australia 2017 National Conference.
33. Beheshti, N. (2018, November 20). Benefits Of A Year-Round Attitude Of Gratitude In The Workplace. *Forbes*. https://www.forbes.com/sites/nazbeheshti/2018/11/20/benefits-of-a-year-round-attitude-of-gratitude-in-the-workplace/#74188f731bc5
34. Newman, K.M. (2017). How Gratitude Can Transform Your Workplace. *Greater Good Magazine*. https://greatergood.berkeley.edu/article/item/how_gratitude_can_transform_your_workplace
35. Waters, L. (2012). Predicting Job Satisfaction: Contributions of Individual Gratitude and Institutionalized Gratitude. *Psychology*, 03 (12), 1174–1176. https://doi.org/10.4236/psych.2012.312a173
36. Limeade Institute. (2019). The Science of Care Whitepaper. *Limeade Institute*. https://www.limeade.com/wp-content/uploads/2019/09/LimeadeInstitute_TheScienceOfCare_Whitepaper_Web.pdf
37. McCarthy, W. (2000). *Don't Fence Me In*. Random House Australia.
38. McCarthy, W. (2022). *Don't Be Too Polite, Girls: A memoir*. Allen & Unwin.

39. Bullock, B. G. (2016). *Mindful Relationships: Seven skills for success.* Handspring Publishing.
40. Bullock, B. G. (2021, February 11). *How to stop your stories from running your life.* https://www.gracebullock.com/post/how-to-stop-your-stories-from-running-your-life-2
41. Eurich, T. (2018). *Insight: The surprising truth about how others see us, how we see ourselves, and why the answers matter more than we think.* Currency.
42. Eurich, T. (2017, June 14). Are You A Self-aware Leader? [Podcast]. *Knowledge at Wharton.* https://knowledge.wharton.upenn.edu/article/going-wise-helps-us-make-smarter-decisions/
43. Berry, S. (2021, September 4). Ash Barty's mindset coach asks these three questions for success. *The Sydney Morning Herald.* https://www.smh.com.au/lifestyle/health-and-wellness/ash-barty-s-mindset-coach-asks-these-three-questions-for-success-20210831-p58nhc.html
44. Trioli, V. (2022, January 31). Mornings with Virginia Trioli. [Radio]. *Australian Broadcasting Network.* https://www.abc.net.au/radio/melbourne/programs/mornings/ash-barty-mindset-coach/13734068
45. Docter, P., & Del Carmen, R. (2015). *Inside Out.* [Movie]. Walt Disney Studios Motion Pictures.
46. Brown, B. (2021). *Atlas of the Heart.* New York Random House.
47. The University of Queensland. (n.d.). A leader's guide to managing emotions at work. *Momentum — the Business School Magazine.* https://business.uq.edu.au/momentum/leaders-guide-managing-emotions-work
48. David, S. (2016, November 10). 3 Ways to Better Understand Your Emotions. *Harvard Business Review.* https://hbr.org/2016/11/3-ways-to-better-understand-your-emotions
49. Maxwell, J. C. (2010). *Everyone Communicates, Few Connect: What the most effective people do differently.* Thomas Nelson.

50. Available to buy from the Intelligent Change website, https://www.intelligentchange.com/products/the-five-minute-journal
51. Deloitte Millennial Survey. (2018). Millennials disappointed in business, unprepared for Industry 4.0. *Deloitte*. https://www2.deloitte.com/content/dam/Deloitte/global/Documents/About-Deloitte/gx-2018-millennial-survey-report.pdf
52. https://www.gallup.com/cliftonstrengths
53. There are many options when it comes to doing an Enneagram test. I used Truity https://www.truity.com/test/enneagram-personality-test
54. https://www.kolbe.com/
55. Porter, J. (2017, June 25). Why You Should Make Time for Self-Reflection (Even If You Hate Doing It). *Harvard Business Review*. https://hbr.org/2017/03/why-you-should-make-time-for-self-reflection-even-if-you-hate-doing-it
56. Schootstra, E., Deichmann, D., & Dolgova, E. (2017, August 29). Can 10 Minutes of Meditation Make You More Creative? *Harvard Business Review*. https://hbr.org/2017/08/can-10-minutes-of-meditation-make-you-more-creative
57. Trimboli, O. (2017). *Deep Listening: impact beyond words*. Trimboli.
58. Holmes, R. (2019, February 20). We Now See 5,000 Ads A Day ... And It's Getting Worse. *LinkedIn*. https://www.linkedin.com/pulse/have-we-reached-peak-ad-social-media-ryan-holmes/
59. Gino, F. (2018, September 1). The Business Case for Curiosity. *Harvard Business Review*. https://hbr.org/2018/09/the-business-case-for-curiosity#the-business-case-for-curiosity
60. Madsen, S. R. (2008). *On Becoming a Woman Leader: learning from the experiences of university presidents*. Jossey-Bass.
61. Raz, G. (Host). (2016, September 12). Spanx: Sara Blakely (No. 1) [Podcast]. *How I Built This with Guy Raz Podcast*. NPR. https://www.npr.org/2017/06/07/493169696/spanx-sara-blakely

62. Lamott, A. (1997). *Bird by Bird.* Anchor Books.
63. Duhigg, C. (2014). *The Power of Habit: Why we do what we do in life and business.* Random House Trade Paperbacks.)
64. Ferriss, T. (Host). (2018, June 4). Morning Routines and Strategies (No. 253) [Podcast]. *The Tim Ferriss Show.* https://tim.blog/2018/06/04/the-tim-ferriss-show-transcripts-morning-routines-and-strategies/
65. Eyal, N. & Li-Eyal, J. (2019). *Indistractable: how to control your attention and choose your life.* Benbella Books.
66. Amabile, T. M., & Kramer, S. J. (2016, June 8). The Power of Small Wins. *Harvard Business Review.* https://hbr.org/2011/05/the-power-of-small-wins
67. Merry, W., Jaerling, S., Prowse-Bishop, L., & Hamlet, S. (2014). *Get More Inspiration: Unexpected ideas to help you achieve.* Get More.
68. Fogg, B. J. (2020). *Tiny Habits: The small changes that change everything.* Mariner Books.
69. Available from http://www.thelaststraw.ca/
70. Warrell, M. (2015, March 17). Six Things Lucky People Do That Others Don't. *Forbes.* https://www.forbes.com/sites/margiewarrell/2015/03/17/create-the-luck-youve-been-wishing-for/?sh=685937294ace
71. Wiseman, R. (2004). *The Luck Factor.* Arrow Books.
72. Covey, S. R. (2013). *7 Habits Of Highly Effective People.* Simon & Schuster.
73. Sinek, S. (2009). *Start With Why: How great leaders inspire everyone to take action.* Portfolio.
74. Dweck, C. (2012). *Mindset: How you can fulfil your potential.* Robinson.
75. Dweck, C. (2014, November). The power of believing that you can improve. *TED Talks.* https://www.ted.com/talks/carol_dweck_the_power_of_believing_that_you_can_improve?language=en

76. Burke, C. (2022). *Lead In: Mindsets to lead, live and work differently*. Burke.
77. Davis, S. (2018, July 18). LeBron James reportedly spends $1.5 million per year to take care of his body — here's where it goes. *Insider Inc.* https://www.businessinsider.com.au/how-lebron-james-spends-money-body-care-2018-7
78. Neff, K. (2015). *Self compassion: stop beating yourself up and leave insecurity behind*. Yellow Kite.
79. https://blacksmith.co.nz/
80. Dogan, V. (2019). Why Do People Experience the Fear of Missing Out (FoMO)? Exposing the Link Between the Self and the FoMO Through Self-Construal. *Journal of Cross-Cultural Psychology*, 50(4), 002202211983914. https://doi.org/10.1177/0022022119839145
81. American Psychological Association. (2012, January 1). Building Your Resilience. *American Psychological Association.* https://www.apa.org/topics/resilience
82. Johnson, K. (2021, May 12). Indoor plant sales boom due to COVID-19, says nursery industry. *Australian Broadcasting Corporation.* https://www.abc.net.au/news/rural/2021-05-12/nursery-owners-notice-a-boom-in-indoor-plant-sales/100130200
83. Mayo Clinic. Mayo Clinic Discovers A Key To 'Low Metabolism' – And Major Factor In Obesity. (2005). *Science Daily.* https://www.sciencedaily.com/releases/2005/01/050128224400.htm
84. Sleep Health Foundation. (2017). Asleep on the job: Costs of inadequate sleep in Australia. *Sleep Health Foundation.* https://www.sleephealthfoundation.org.au/files/Asleep_on_the_job/Asleep_on_the_Job_SHF_report-WEB_small.pdf
85. Molloy, S. (2018, August 15). Australians aren't getting enough sleep, and it's slowly killing you. *The Courier Mail.* https://www.couriermail.com.au/lifestyle/health/australians-arent-getting-enough-sleep-and-its-slowly-killing-you/news-story/1619d1e0b1ddf556a811d92cb33ba0f0?

86. Jabr, F. (2013, October 15). Why Your Brain Needs More Downtime. *Scientific American*. https://www.scientificamerican.com/article/mental-downtime/
87. Branson, R. (2013, September 3). Your inspiration vacation. *Mint*. https://www.livemint.com/Opinion/1hs6w0ys4xpq8jBA8VNFsI/Your-inspiration-vacation.html
88. Sivers, D. (2020). Hell yeah or no: what's worth doing. Hit Media.

www.ingramcontent.com/pod-product-compliance
Lightning Source LLC
Chambersburg PA
CBHW050758160426
43192CB00010B/1566